Sir Richard Burton's Travels in Arabia and Africa

Four Lectures from a Huntington Library Manuscript

Sir Richard F. Burton. From Isabel Burton, *The Inner Life of Syria, Palestine, and the Holy Land* (1875).

Sir Richard Burton's Travels in Arabia and Africa

Four Lectures from a Huntington Library Manuscript

edited by John Hayman

Huntington Library
San Marino, California

Published by Huntington Library Press
1151 Oxford Road, San Marino, CA 91108
http://www.huntington.org

Cover illustration: Sir Richard F. Burton. From Isabel Burton,
The Inner Life of Syria, Palestine, and the Holy Land (1875).
Cover design by Doug Davis

Library of Congress Catalog Card No. 90044363

Burton, Richard Francis, Sir, 1821–1890.
    Sir Richard Burton's travels in Arabia and Africa : four
lectures from a Huntington Library manuscript / edited by John Hayman.
        109 p. ill., maps ; 27 cm.
Includes bibliographical references.
ISBN: 0-87328-209-4
1. Burton, Richard Francis, Sir, 1821–1890—Travel—Saudi Arabia—Medina.
2. Burton, Richard Francis, Sir, 1821–1890—Travel—Saudi Arabia—Mecca. 3. Burton,
Richard Francis, Sir, 1821–1890—Travel—Somalia. 4. Burton, Richard Francis, Sir,
1821–1890—Travel—Benin. 5. Medina (Saudi Arabia)—Description and travel.
6. Mecca (Saudi Arabia)—Description and travel. 7. Somalia—Description and
travel. 8. Benin—Description and travel. I. Hayman, John, 1935– . II. Henry E.
Huntington Library and Art Gallery.
DS248.M5 B873 1990
915.3804'4'092—B 20

Contents

Illustrations

The book illustrations reproduced here were originally based on drawings by Burton.

Introduction

In 1886, at the age of sixty-five, Richard Burton (1821-90) requested that he be allowed to retire from the consular service on a full pension, and in his appeal to the authorities he outlined his "services":

1. Served nineteen years in the Bombay Army, nearly ten years on active service, chiefly on the staff of Sir Charles Napier, on the Sind Survey, at the close of the Afghan War, 1842-9. In 1861 was compelled to leave, without pay or pension, by Sir Charles Wood, for accepting the Consulship of Fernando Po.
2. Served in the Crimea as Chief of the Staff of Bashi-Bazouk (Irregular Cavalry), and was chiefly instrumental in organizing it.
3. Was the author of the Bayonet Exercise now used at the Horseguards.
4. Have made several difficult and dangerous expeditions or explorations in unknown parts; notably the pilgrimage to Mecca and Medinah, and afterwards to Harar, now opened up to Europeans, and the discovery and opening up of the Lake Regions of Central Africa, and the sources of the Nile, a country now well known to trade, to missionaries, and schoolmasters.
5. Have been twenty-five years and a half in the Consular Service, eight to nine years in official bad climates.
6. Was sent in 1864, as H.M.'s Commissioner to the King of Dahomé, and resided with him for three months.
7. Was recalled at a moment's notice from Damascus [when consul there], under a misrepresentation, and suffered heavy pecuniary losses thereby. My conduct was at last formally approved by the Government, but no compensation was given. . . .
9. Have learned twenty-nine languages, passed official examinations in eight Eastern languages, notably Arabic, Persian, and Hindustani.
10. Have published over forty-six works, several of which, like 'Mecca,' and the 'Exploration of Harar,' are now standard.[1]

The list of activities is impressive, but Burton might well have extended it. He did not mention his poetry, his anthropological inquiries, or his translation and publication of erotica. It is understandable, how-

---

1 Isabel Burton, *The Life of Captain Sir Richd. F. Burton* (London, 1893), 1:325.

ever, that he should have left these activities unmentioned. His most ambitious poem, *Stone Talk* (1865), was fiercely critical of government officials and prevailing social attitudes. His anthropological writings, especially when concerned with sexual practices, had sometimes been suppressed, even when he had decently cloaked them in Latin. His translations of erotica were in part acts of bravado—both a rejection of conventional morality and a way of exposing the true taste and moral values of the reading public.

Burton's activity as a lecturer also goes unnoticed in his autobiographical outline, but this again is not surprising, since apart from his specialized papers to such organizations as the Royal Geographical Society and the Anthropological Society, he seems not to have gone in much for public address. The lectures presented here also had a specialized audience—and an improbable venue. They were written in 1866, during the period when Burton was consul in Brazil (1865-69), and delivered there before a distinguished audience. In a letter to her mother of June 1866, Isabel Burton wrote, presumably midway through the series: "Richard has given two lectures before a room full of people. The Emperor and Empress, Comte d'Eu, and Princesse Impériale were present."[2] Burton clearly kept the needs and interests of this audience in mind, providing it with some very basic geographical information and some engaging comparisons between South America and other parts of the world.

Burton's procedures in composing the lectures vary. Lectures 1 and 2 are skillful abridgments of *Personal Narrative of a Pilgrimage to El-Medinah and Meccah* (1855) and often follow the more detailed account word for word. Lectures 3 and 4 relate to the book-length accounts *First Footsteps in East Africa* (1856) and *A Mission to Gelele, King of Dahome* (1864), but they do not follow the detailed versions so closely. Inevitably, the lectures lack many of the vivid particulars of the more extended accounts. But even Burton's contemporaries often found his multivolume publications rather prolix. The lectures succinctly introduce some of his major achievements.

Apart from his quest for the source of the Nile, Burton is probably remembered most often for his penetration of the Islamic shrines at Medina (Lecture 1) and Mecca (Lecture 2). These were escapades which had all the characteristics of high adventure: an exotic location, deliberate

---

2 W. H. Wilkins, *The Romance of Isabel Lady Burton* (New York, 1908), 260.

preparation, disguise, setbacks, hardship and danger. In addition, Burton was animated by a genuine interest in Islamic practices and beliefs which enabled him to enter imaginatively into the experience of a pilgrimage. The account of his journey to Harar in East Africa (Lecture 3) is more simply a tale of adventure, but even here there are some ethnological considerations which add significance to the account. This is also true of the lecture on his visit to Dahomey (Lecture 4), although his assumption of racial superiority of course invalidates many of his ethnographic generalizations. Together, these journeys resulted in some of Burton's more rewarding travel books, and the lectures convey much of their merit.

In addition, the lectures reveal much about Burton's personality and temperament. Each of the lectures displays, for example, a restless spirit which may be related to the unsettled years of Burton's childhood. His father had been an army man who became accustomed to a life abroad while serving in Italy. This inclination to live on the Continent was further encouraged after he fell out of favor in England as a result of his refusal to testify against Queen Caroline when George IV wished to divorce her. Burton said of his father's conduct on this occasion that he "behaved like a gentleman"[3]—a remark which shows that conventional moral evaluation sometimes accompanied Burton's rebellious attitudes. When Burton was a few months old, the family settled near Tours, where there resided an extensive English colony. Expatriates, these families also seemed to Burton to be "intensely patriotic" (1:18)—a paradox which may be related to Burton's own personality perhaps as readily as to the society of Tours itself. It was also this nationalism which resulted in the family's returning to England for the education of their children, though to Burton the school he and his brother attended seemed "a kind of Dotheboys Hall," in which the headmaster was "no more fit to be a schoolmaster than the Great Cham of Tartary" (1:28). When an epidemic of measles struck the school, the family again set out on its travels, with sojourns at Blois, Lyons, Marseilles, Pau, Pisa, Siena, Florence, Rome, and Naples. These travels enabled Burton to develop his gift for languages, which he was later to turn to advantage. Similarly, his later explorations may be seen as attempts to turn to good account a restlessness that was communicated to him at an early age.

---

3   Isabel Burton, *Life of Burton*, 1:17. Quotations in this and the following paragraph are from the part of Isabel Burton's biography which she describes as "copied from his private Journals." Page references are included in the text.

At an early age he also learned the value of disguise. He was fifteen when an outbreak of cholera devastated Naples during the family's sojourn there. In a defiant show of unconcern about his safety and with an equally characteristic display of curiosity, Burton apparently arranged with his brother that they should be disguised as undertakers' mutes, and they assisted the men who carried out mass burials of the poor. In a macabre description of the procedure, he was later to write of the naked bodies being committed to the communal grave. "Black and rigid," he wrote, "they were thrown . . . like so much rubbish, into the festering heap below, and the decay caused a kind of lambent blue flame about the sides of the pit, which lit up a mass of human corruption, worthy to be described by Dante" (1:51-52).

On other occasions, disguise had a more comic role; it appealed to Burton's sense of drama and ingenuity. In *Goa, and the Blue Mountains; or, Six Months of Sick Leave* (London, 1851), he is almost certainly thinking of himself when he has Salvador describe the escapades of his master, an unnamed Lieutenant. "He could talk to each man of a multitude in his own language," Salvador reports, "and all of them would appear equally surprised by, and delighted with him. Besides, his faith was every man's faith. . . . He chaunted the Koran, and the circumcised dogs considered him a kind of saint. The Hindoos also respected him, because he always ate his beef in secret, and had a devil (i.e., some heathen image) in an inner room. At Cochin he went to the Jewish place of worship, and read a large book, just like a priest. Ah! he was a clever Sahib that."[4] Salvador is speaking of an officer in the Indian service, and it was during Burton's service in India (1842-49) that he gained knowledge of local life by disguising himself as "half-Arab, half-Iranian, such as may be met with in thousands along the northern shore of the Persian Gulf."[5]

Three of the lectures that follow reveal Burton's adeptness in arranging disguise. His pilgrimages to Mecca and Medina were distinguished, Burton claimed, by his successful disguise as one born into the Islamic faith. Burton remarked that he knew only one other adventurer who had adopted this strategy—Bertolucci, the Swedish consul at Cairo—and he noted that Bertolucci had been so terrified of being discovered that he had been unable to observe at all closely. Others who had penetrated the mosques commemorating the birth and death of the prophet had done so as "converts," and they had consequently been given special treatment.

---

4 *Goa, and the Blue Mountains,* 74.
5 Isabel Burton, *Life of Burton,* 1:155.

As Burton and others remarked, his personal appearance made possible his disguise as an Arab. Alfred Bates Richards, an Oxford friend, was later to comment: "The Eastern, and indeed distinctly Arab, look of the man is made more pronounced by prominent cheek-bones (across one of which is the scar of a sabre-cut), by closely-cropped black hair just tinged with gray, and a pair of piercing black, gipsy-looking eyes. . . . It is not to be wondered at that this stern Arab face, and a tongue marvellously rich in Oriental idiom and Mahometan lore, should have deceived the doctors learned in the Koran."[6] Burton also made meticulous preparations for the pilgrimage—even to the extent of undergoing circumcision.

Above all, his strategy of disguise compelled him to observe the daily conduct of Arab life with precision. The result is such detailed and vivid description as this:

> Look, for instance, at that Indian Moslem drinking a glass of water. With us the operation is simple enough, but his performance includes no fewer than five novelties. In the first place he clutches his tumbler as though it were the throat of a foe; secondly, he ejaculates, "In the name of Allah the Compassionate, the Merciful!" before wetting his lips; thirdly, he imbibes the contents, swallowing them, not sipping them as he ought to do, and ending with a satisfied grunt; fourthly, before setting down the cup, he sighs forth, "Praise be to Allah!"—of which you will understand the full meaning in the Desert; and fifthly, he replies, "May Allah make it pleasant to thee!" in answer to his friend's polite "Pleasurably and health!"[7]

It was rumored in Burton's lifetime that he was forced to kill an Arab who had seen him urinate in a standing position, rather than in the crouched position of the Middle East. Burton denied the truth of this story, and it is surely difficult to imagine that so vigilant an observer could have been guilty of such a dangerous lapse.

Burton was also resourceful in changing his disguise when this proved necessary. On his pilgrimage to Mecca, he discovered that his choice of a Persian character had been unfortunate, and so he became a "Pathan, born in India of Afghan parents."[8] Similarly, for the expedition

---

6 *A Sketch of the Career of Richard F. Burton* (London, 1886), 33.
7 *Personal Narrative of a Pilgrimage to Al-Madinah & Meccah* (Memorial edition, London, 1893), 1:6.
8 *Personal Narrative of a Pilgrimage*, 1:145.

to Harar, he took on again his disguise as an Arabian pilgrim, but he finally threw off this disguise and adopted a quasi-official role as a British emissary.

Burton's disguises were, then, considered strategies, and yet they seem only partly explained by practical considerations. For Burton rather obviously found pleasure in shocking Victorian propriety by taking on as a pilgrim both the dress and the character of an "infidel." He could be incensed, too, by the unchangeableness of the English—as represented, for example, by his fellow-explorer and subsequent antagonist, John Hanning Speke. In *What Led to the Discovery of the Source of the Nile* (1864), Speke wrote that he was urged to adopt Arab dress "in order to attract less attention." Speke, however, refused to lower himself. "I was more comfortable and better off," he wrote, "in my flannel shirt, long togs, and wide-awake, than I should have been, both mentally and physically, had I degraded myself."[9] In his copy of Speke's book (now in the Huntington, Burton Library no. 1680), Burton has underlined the latter part of this sentence and scribbled in the margin: "Rot." He was equally vigorous in his response to the "truculent attacks" made upon him for taking on the role of a pilgrim.[10]

His choice of a specific character also deserves close scrutiny. In particular, the role of a "darwaysh" (or dervish) which he adopted for his pilgrimage to Mecca and Medina arranged a license which suited his wayward and unpredictable responses:

> No character in the Moslem world [Burton wrote] is so proper for disguise as that of the Darwaysh. It is assumed by all ranks, ages, and creeds; by the nobleman who has been disgraced at court, and by the peasant who is too idle to till the ground; by Dives, who is weary of life, and by Lazarus, who begs his bread from door to door. . . . He may pray or not, marry or remain single as he pleases, be respectable in cloth of frieze as in cloth of gold, and no one asks him—the chartered vagabond—Why he comes here? or Wherefore he goes there? He may wend his way on foot alone, or ride his Arab mare followed by a dozen servants; he is equally feared without weapons, as swaggering through the streets armed to the teeth. The more haughty and offensive he is to people, the more they respect him; a decided advantage to the traveller of choleric temperament.[11]

9 *Discovery of the Source of the Nile*, 314.
10 "Preface to the Third Edition," *Personal Narrative of a Pilgrimage* (1879), 1:xx.
11 *Personal Narrative of a Pilgrimage*, 1:14-15.

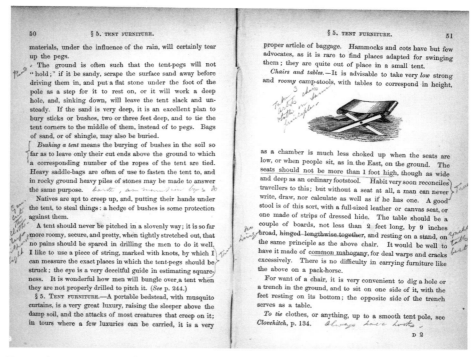

Burton's preparations for travel included annotating Francis Galton's *Art of Travel*. From Burton Library no. 38, in the Huntington Library.

In this final, sly aside, it seems that Burton is aware how temperamentally suited the role is for him. As Lady Burton remarked, "He went to Cairo as a dervish, and he lived there as a native, till (as he told me) he actually believed himself to be what he represented himself to be."[12]

The dervish, then, was a wayward character—but the successful adoption of such a character also called for discipline and control. Burton did not always find it possible to summon these qualities of character. In *Personal Narrative of a Pilgrimage* he writes, for example, of having rather hastily to leave Cairo as a result of a disreputable brawl. But such incidents were rare, and Burton benefited from the enforced discipline of his chosen role. His life, as his summary of it indicated, was characterized above all by the variousness of his activities. He was equally a man of action and a man of letters. The volatile changes of his moods sometimes bewildered him: the movement from passiveness to assertion, from sensual indulgence to intellectual activity, from lying in a hammock and

12 Isabel Burton, *Life of Burton*, 1:169.

staring into the clear sky to pressing forward in the heat of the day. In an extraordinarily revealing comment on the effect of a rootless upbringing, he remarked: "You are a waif, a stray; you are a blaze of light, without a focus."[13] A disguise, especially when the lapse from it might bring about death, wonderfully concentrated the mind.

The inherent danger of disguise was also part of the appeal. Burton's delight in challenge amounted to defiance. As he remarked: "Man's heart bounds in his breast at the thought of measuring his puny force with Nature's might, and of emerging triumphant from the trial."[14] The danger of the pilgrimage to Mecca and Medina has always been recognized, but as his wife remarked, the journey to Harar was also "one of Richard's most splendid and dangerous expeditions,"[15] and the same might be claimed for the expedition to Dahomey. The appeal of such locations was precisely that they were forbidden.

Such defiance seems always to have been a part of Burton's make-up. In some autobiographical reminiscences, for example, he wrote of his mother's aiming to present "a wholesome and moral lesson" by having him, his brother, and his sister admire some French pastries in a shop window—and then pass on. "Upon this," Burton writes, "we three devilets turned flashing eyes and burning cheeks upon our moralizing mother, broke the windows with our fists, clawed out the tray of apple-puffs, and bolted, leaving our poor mother a sadder and wiser woman, to pay the damages of her lawless brood's proceedings"(1:22). It is the extraordinary violence of the response—whether the recollection is of an actual or an imagined event—that is so remarkable here. The deliberate descent to an animal existence could scarcely be better expressed than by the reference to clawing and bolting.

As an undergraduate at Oxford, Burton was equally defiant. His scattered education had ill prepared him for Trinity College, which he entered in 1840 at the age of nineteen. In particular, he had developed some linguistic idiosyncrasies which he unwisely flaunted before authorities and colleagues. "They laughed at me, at my first lecture," he later recalled, "because I spoke in Roman Latin—real Latin—I did not know the English pronunciation, only known in England"(1:79). In this Burton was finally to be vindicated, as he was on other occasions; the English

---

13 Ibid., 32.
14 *Personal Narrative of a Pilgrimage*, 1:149.
15 Isabel Burton, *Life of Burton*, 1:199. Quotations in the next three paragraphs are from this source.

turned from their peculiar pronunciation. In dictating his autobiography, Burton was to acknowledge his perversity, and he was again to refer to his being possessed by a devilish inclination. "The devil palpably entered into me," he remarked, "and made me speak Greek Romaically by accent, and not by quantity, even as they did and still do at Athens" (1:83). Finally, in order to arrange that he be sent down, Burton had to defy the authorities more flagrantly. Against orders, he attended some horse races, and he compounded the outrage by going in a forbidden vehicle—a tandem. Accordingly, he was rusticated with "an especial recommendation not to return" (1:90). He arranged that a tandem should come to the college for him, and after driving over the college flower beds, he set out for London. Of tandems themselves, he remarked: "No one would have driven them had they not possessed the merits of stolen fruit" (1:78).

By his own account, Burton arranged that he should be rusticated in order to persuade his father that he should be permitted to enter the army. In this, he was also defying his father's intentions. A disappointed military man, Burton's father was determined that neither of his sons should enter the army—"the consequence being," Burton remarked, "that both the sons became soldiers" (1:50). Later, his pursuit of Isabel Arundel, whom he finally married, was in defiance of her parents. In all these instances, Burton defied "authorities," and this attitude was also to characterize his official career both in the army and as a consul. His lectures refer several times to clashes with government officials and officers of the East India Company. On occasion, Burton even admitted to some perversity about his attitudes. "The devil drives," he wryly remarked, when reflecting on his motivation.[16] On other occasions, he involved his defiance within tangled claims of moral superiority. In his lectures, however, he is not intent on either self-justification or self-accusation—nor is he intent on attacking authorities. With members of the royal family of Brazil in his audience that would clearly have been inappropriate. As consul, he had an official position to maintain. As lecturer, he assumed the role of an authoritative and assured citizen of the world.

------

16 The phrase forms the title for the excellent biography of Burton by Fawn M. Brodie (New York, 1967). She has taken it from a letter of Burton to Monckton Milnes (Lord Houghton), quoted on p. 15.

The first page of Lecture 3, reproduced from the Huntington Library manuscript (HM 27955).

Note on the Text

The holograph of the lectures presented here is in a blue-covered book (10⁵/₈ x 8¹/₈ inches) in the Huntington Library (HM 27955). A version of the lectures was published, together with other material, in *Wanderings on Three Continents*, edited by W. H. Wilkins (London, 1901). However, Wilkins's deletions and alterations were very extensive, even though he acknowledged only the deletion of "the local and topical allusions, which arose from the circumstances under which [the lectures] were delivered" (p. vii). He omits, for example, the opening six pages of "First Footsteps in Eastern Africa," in which Burton provides a valuable summary of both earlier notions about Africa and recent discoveries. Similarly, he omits the opening ten pages of "A Mission to Dahome," in which Burton distinguishes among different African tribes and outlines his attitude towards slavery. Even more capriciously, Wilkins includes the passage in "A Mission to Dahome" in which Burton promises a "panacea" for the "hopeless misery" of the African—and then deletes the "panacea." In the present edition, the complete text of the lectures is presented.

Wilkins's version of the lectures is also marred by many inaccurate transcriptions. Perhaps the most outlandish is his rendering of a 7.5-mile journey as 7,500 miles. Admittedly, Burton's handwriting can be problematic—the result, one imagines, of his scribbling in haste on tiny pieces of paper in countries where the written word was regarded with suspicion. The text of the lectures is, however, relatively clear, perhaps because Burton wished to avoid stumbling over his own handwriting.

In transcribing the text, I have occasionally clarified Burton's abbreviations and punctuation. To avoid a plethora of footnotes, I have included some explanatory material within squared brackets in the text. In all other respects, I have followed Burton's text exactly.

I wish to thank Alan Jutzi, Susan Hodson, Guilland Sutherland, and Susan Green of the Huntington Library for the encouragement and assistance they provided throughout my work on this edition. I am also grateful to Diane Rutherford for her careful typing of the manuscript.

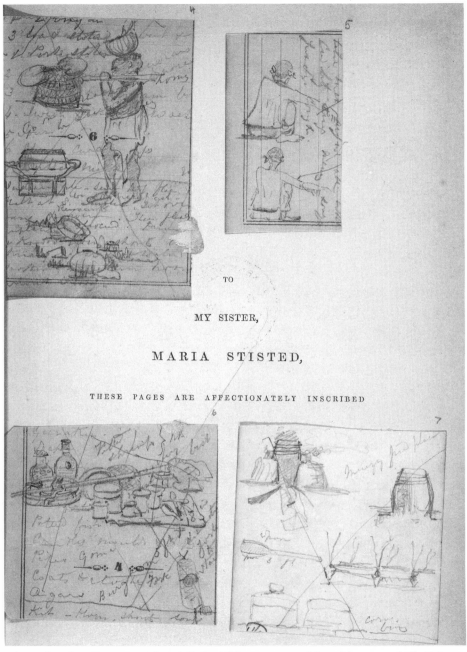

These sketches Burton made while in Africa are pasted into his copy of *The Lake Regions of Central Africa* (Burton Library no. 10). Burton had to be circumspect when taking notes or making sketches on his travels since the activity might be associated with spying. In *Personal Narrative of a Pilgrimage,* he remarked: "For prudence sake, when my sketches were made, I cut up the paper into square pieces, numbered them for future reference, and hid them in the tin canisters that contained my medicines" (1:240n).

Lectures 1 & 2
The Visitation at El Medinah &
The Pilgrimage to Meccah
Introduction

Burton's pilgrimage to Medina and Mecca at the age of thirty-two was the first of his major expeditions, and it has remained one of his most celebrated. The three-volume account of it, which appeared in 1855 under the title *Personal Narrative of a Pilgrimage to El-Medinah and Meccah*, remains in print.

Burton himself did not, however, make great claims for his expedition, perhaps because he had initially planned a much more ambitious enterprise. He readily acknowledged that other Europeans had previously penetrated the shrines at Mecca and Medina, and he meticulously remarked on their accounts. His own claim as a pilgrim was that he had traveled as one born into the faith, rather than as a convert or as an infidel under the guardianship of a Moslem. In his reliance on a hazardous disguise, Burton displayed his characteristic daring.

Burton was also modest about his account of the pilgrimage, claiming only that it was more detailed than the accounts of his predecessors. However, Burton's distinctive personality colors even the abbreviated account in his lecture. In particular, the volatile changes of mood and feeling which characterize Burton are associated in his account with the pilgrimage itself. Chaotic activity alternates with religious discipline. The caravan of religious pilgrims is attacked by brigands. It passes through both the "Country of Date Trees" and the "Salt Stony Land." The terrain offers both "the face of a friend" and the threat of death. Burton's restless spirit clearly reveled in such contrasts.

The reference to a "personal narrative" in the title of Burton's three-volume account of the pilgrimage suggests that he was aware that the individuality and daring of his enterprise would appeal to his readers. In his lectures, however, he did not wish to appear egotistical, and near the opening of his first lecture he tactfully apologized for its autobiographical concern. The "personal" was to be contained within the persona of a scholarly lecturer and urbane man of the world. This arrangement of a persona, like all Burton's guises, was of course a calculated performance —even to the point of his writing into the script his thanks for the "friendly attention" of the audience.

Lecture 1
The Visitation at El Medinah

The Moslem's Pilgrimage is a familiar word to the Christian's ear, yet how few are acquainted with the nature or the significance of the rite. Unto the present day, learned men (for instance Mr. Halliwell editing Sir John Mandeville) still confound Meccah, the birthplace, with El Medinah, the burial-place, of Mohammed, the Arab law-giver.[1] "The Prophet's tomb at Meccah" is a mistake which even the best-informed of our journals do not disdain to make. I venture to say that those who kindly give ear to me tonight will never fall into this popular error.

Before, however, entering upon the journey which procured for me the title of "Haji" [pilgrim], it is necessary to dispose of a few preliminaries which must savour of the personal. I hope you will not say of the egotistical. The first question that suggests itself to my hearer is, "What course of study enabled an Englishman to pass unsuspected through the Moslem's exclusive and jealously-guarded Holy Land?"

I need hardly remark that in the matter of assuming an Oriental nationality, Nature has been somewhat propitious to me: golden locks and blue eyes, however per se desirable, would have been sad obstacles to progress in swarthy Arabia. And to what Nature had begun, Art contributed by long years of laborious occupation.

Finding Oxford, with its Greek and Latin, its mysteries of ψαρ and δε, and its theology and mathematics, exceedingly monotonous, I shipped myself for India and entered life in the 18th Sepoy Regiment of the Bombay Presidency. With sundry intervals of travel, my career between 1843 and 1849 was spent in Sindh. This newly conquered province was very Mohammedan, and the conquerors were compelled, during the work of organization, to see more of the conquered than is usual in England's East Indian possessions. Sir Charles Napier of gallant memory, our Governor and Commander-in-Chief, honoured me with a staff appointment, and humoured my whim by allowing me to wander about the new land as an engineer employed upon its intricate canal system. My days and nights were thus spent amongst the people, and with-

---

1   J. O. Halliwell contributed an introduction, additional notes, and a glossary to a reprint of the 1725 edition of Sir John Mandeville's *Voyages and Travels* (1839). In *Personal Narrative of a Pilgrimage,* Burton remarked that Mandeville referred to Methone (Meccah) as the burial place of Mohammed (1:286n).

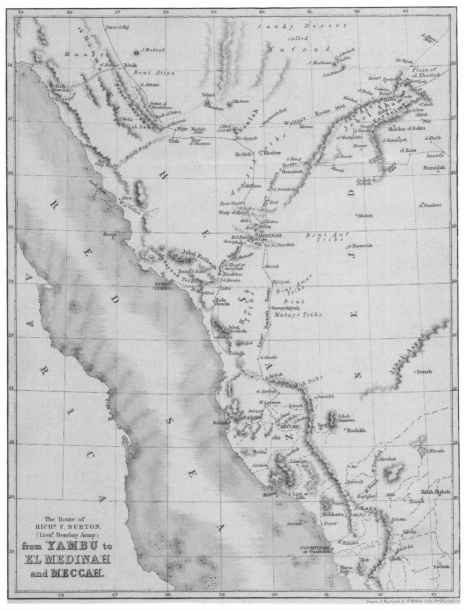

Route from Yambu to El Medinah and Mecca. From *Personal Narrative of a Pilgrimage to El-Medinah and Meccah* (1855).

in five years I was enabled to pass examinations in six Eastern languages.[2]

In 1849 (March 30th-September 5th) an obstinate rheumatic ophthalmia, the result of overwork, sent me to Europe, where nearly three years were passed before I was pronounced cured. Then, thoroughly tired of civilization and of living "dully sluggardised at home,"[3] and pining for the breath of the Desert and the music of the date-palm, I volunteered in the autumn of 1852 to explore the Great Waste of Eastern and Central Arabia, that huge white blot which still disgraces our best maps. But the then Court of Directors to the then Honourable East India Company, with their mild and amiable chairman, Sir James Hogg, stoutly refused. They saw in me only another victim, like Stoddart, Conolly, and the brave brothers Wyburd,[4] rushing on his own destruction and leaving behind him friends and family to trouble with their requisitions the peace and quiet of the India House.

What remained to me but to prove that what might imperil others was to me safe? Supplied with the sinews of travel by the Royal Geographical Society of Great Britain; curious to see what men are mostly content only to hear of—namely, Moslem inner life in a purely Mohammedan land—and longing to set foot within that mysterious Meccah which no vacation tourist has yet measured, sketched, photographed, and described, I resolved, *coûte que coûte,* to make the attempt in my old character of a Dervish. The safest as well as the most interesting time would be during the Pilgrimage-Season.

The Moslem's hajj, or Pilgrimage, means, I must premise, "aspiration," and expresses man's conviction that he is but a wayfarer on earth wending towards a nobler world. This explains the general belief of the men in sandalled shoon, that the greater their hardships, the sorer to travel the road to Jordan, the higher will be their reward in heaven. The pilgrim is urged by the voice of his soul—"O thou, toiling so fiercely for worldly pleasure and for transitory profit, wilt thou endure nothing to win a more lasting boon?" Hence it is that pilgrimage was common to all

---

2 In the autobiographical section of Isabel Burton's *Life of Burton,* the following languages are specified: Hindostani (1:120), Gujarati (1:122, 124), Maharátta (1:129, 155), Sindi (1:151), Panjábi (1:151), and Persian (1:155).

3 Shakespeare, *Two Gentlemen of Verona,* act 1, sc. 1, line 7.

4 Colonel Charles Stoddart (b. 1806) and Captain Arthur Conolly (b. 1807) were arrested at Bokhara while on a diplomatic mission. They were probably executed in 1842. I have been unable to find details about the Wyburd brothers.

old Faiths. The Sabaeans or old Arabians visited the Pyramids as the Sepulchres of Seth and his son Sabi, the founder of their sect. The classic philosophers wandered through the Valley of the Nile. The Jews annually went up to Jerusalem. The Tartar Buddhists still journey to distant Lamaserais, and the Hindus to Egypt, to Tibet, to Gaya on the Ganges, and to the inhospitable Caucasus. The spirit of pilgrimage animated mediaeval Europe, and M. Huc, the learned Jesuit traveller [*Travels in Tartary, Tibet, and China* . . . (Paris, 1850; trans. London, 1852)], considers the processions of the Catholic Church modern vestiges of the olden rite.

El Islam—meaning the "covenant in virtue of which men earn eternal life by good works in this world"—requires of all its votaries daily ablution and prayer, almsgiving on certain occasions, one month's yearly fast, and at least one pilgrimage to the House of Allah at Meccah and the mountain of Arafat. This first, and often the single, visit is called Hajjat el Islam, or Pilgrimage of being a Moslem, and all those subsequently performed are regarded as works of supererogation. The rite, however, is incumbent only upon those who possess a sufficiency of health or wealth. El Islam is a creed remarkable for common sense.

The journey to El Medinah is not called hajj, but "ziyarat," meaning a ceremonial visitation: thus the difference between worship due to the Creator and homage rendered to the Creature is steadily placed and kept before the Moslem's eyes. Some sects—the Wahhabi or Arabian Puritans, for instance—even condemn as impious all intercession between man and his Maker, especially the prayers at the Prophet's grave. The mass, however, of the Mohammedan Church, if such expression be applicable to a system which repudiates an ecclesiastical body, considers this visitation a "Practice of the Faith and the most effectual way of drawing near to Allah, through the Prophet Mohammed."

The Moslem's literature has many a thick volume upon the minutiae of Pilgrimage and Visitation: all the four Sunni, or orthodox schools —viz. Hanafi, Shafei, Maliki, and Hanbali—differ in unimportant points one with the other. Usually pilgrims, especially those performing the rite for the first time, begin with Meccah and end with El Medinah. But there is no positive command on the subject. In these days pilgrims from the north countries—Egypt and Syria, Damascus and Bagdad—pass through the Prophet's burial-place going to and coming from Meccah, making a visitation each time. Voyagers from the South—as East Africa, India, and Java—must often deny themselves, on account of its danger and expense, the spiritual advantages of prayer at Mohammed's Tomb.

I have often been asked if the Pilgrim receives any written proof that he has performed his pilgrimage. Formerly the Sharif (descendant of Hasan), or Prince of Meccah gave a certificate to those who could afford it, and early in the present century, the names of all who paid the fee were registered by a scribe. It is not so now. But the ceremonies are so complicated and the localities are so peculiar that no book can thoroughly teach them. The pretended Pilgrim would readily be detected after a short cross-questioning by the real Simon Pure. As facilities of travel increase and the rite becomes more popular, no Pilgrim, unless he come from the edge of the Moslem world, cares to bind on the green turban which his grandfather affected. Few also style themselves Haji, unless for an especial reason—as an evidence of reformed life, for instance, or a sign of being a serious person.

Some friends also have inquired if I am not the first Christian who ever visited the Moslem's Holy Land. So the learned Edward Gibbon (*Decline and Fall of the Roman Empire*, Chapter 50) asserted: "Our notions of Mecca must be drawn from the Arabians: as no unbeliever is permitted to enter the city, our travellers are silent." But Haji Yunus (Ludovico di Bartema) performed the pilgrimage in A.D. 1503; Joseph Pitts, of Exeter, in 1680, Ali Bey el Abbasi (the Catalonian Badia) in 1807, Haji Mohammed (Giovanni Finati, of Ferrara) in 1811, and the excellent Swiss Traveller Burckhardt in 1814 all passed safely through the Hejaz, or Holy Land. I mention those only who have written upon the subject:[5] those who have not must be far more numerous. In fact, any man may become a Haji by prefacing [his pilgrimage] with a solemn and public profession of Faith before the Kazi (judge) in Cairo or Damascus; or, simpler still, by applying through his Consulate to be put under the protection of the Amir el Hajj, or Commander of the Pilgrim Caravan.

If I have done anything new, it is this—my Pilgrimage was performed as by one of the people. El Islam theoretically encourages, but practically despises and distrusts, the Burma, or renegade: such a convert is allowed to see as little as possible and is ever suspected of being a spy. He is carefully watched, night and day, and in troubled times he finds it difficult to travel between Meccah and El Medinah. Far be it from me to disparage the meritorious labours of my predecessors. But

---

5 In appendices to *Personal Narrative of a Pilgrimage,* Burton included passages from the accounts of these travelers (2:333-401).

Bartema travelled as a Mameluke in the days when Mamelukes were Christian slaves, Pitts was a captive carried to the Pilgrimage by his Algierine master, Badia's political position was known to all the authorities, Finati was an Albanian soldier, and Burckhardt revealed himself to the old Pacha Mohammed Ali.

As regards the danger of Pilgrimage in the case of the non-Moslem, little beyond the somewhat extensive chapter of accidents is to be apprehended by one conversant with Moslem prayers and formulas, manners and customs, and who possesses a sufficient guarantee of orthodoxy. It is, however, absolutely indispensable to be a Mohammedan in externals. Neither the Koran nor the Sultan enjoins the killing of Hebrew or Christian intruders; nevertheless, in 1860, a Jew, who refused to repeat the Creed, was crucified by the Meccan populace,[6] and in the event of a pilgrim declaring himself to be an Infidel, the authorities would be powerless to protect him.

The question of *Cui bono?*—of what good I did to others or to myself by the adventure—is not so easily answered. My account of El Medinah is somewhat fuller than that of Burckhardt, whose health was breaking when he visited it. And our caravan's route between the Holy Cities was not the beaten track along the Red Sea, but the little-known eastern or desert road. Some critics certainly twitted me with having "turned Turk"; on the other hand, I have the honour of standing before you and of telling my tale this night, and man is ever most tempted by the useless and by the Impossible.

The Preliminaries are now finished: we will prepare for the journey!

To appear in character upon the scene of action many precautions were necessary. Egypt even twelve years [ago] was a land of passports and policemen; the *haute-police* was not inferior to that of any European country. By the advice of a brother-officer Captain Grindlay, I assumed the Eastern dress at my lodgings in London, and my friend accompanied me as interpreter to Southampton. On the 4th of April 1853, a certain Shaykh Abdullah left home in the P. & O. Company's steamer "Bengal," and before the end of the fortnight made Alexandria. It was not exactly pleasant for the said personage to speak broken English the whole way and rigorously to refuse himself the pleasure of addressing the other sex. But under the circumstances it was necessary.

---

6   Burton is apparently indebted for this information to El Haj Abd El Wahid, whose account of his pilgrimage in 1862 forms appendix 8 in *Personal Narrative of a Pilgrimage,* 2:409-14.

Fortunately, on board the "Bengal" was Mr. John Larking, an old Alexandrian. He was in my secret, and I was received in his house, where he gave me a little detached pavilion and treated me as a munshi, or language-master. My profession amongst the people was that of a doctor. The Egyptians are a medico-ridden race: all are more or less unhealthy, and they could not look upon my phials and pill-boxes without yearning for their contents. An Indian doctor was a novelty to them: Franks they despised but how resist a man who had come so far, from East and West? Men, women, and children besieged my door, by which means I could see the people face to face, especially that portion of which Europeans as a rule know only the worst. Even learned Alexandrians, after witnessing some experiences in Mesmerism and the Magic Mirror,[7] opined that the stranger was a manner of holy man gifted with preternatural powers. An old person sent to offer me his daughter in marriage—my sanctity compelled me to decline the honour. And a middle-aged lady offered me a hundred piastres (nearly one pound sterling) to stay at Alexandria and superintend the restoration of her blind left eye.

After a month pleasantly spent in the little garden of roses, jasmine, and oleanders, I made in early June a move towards Cairo. The first thing was to procure a passport—I had neglected, through ignorance, to bring one from England. It was not without difficulty, involving much unclean dressing and expenditure of horrible English, that I obtained from H.B.M.'s Consul at Alexandria a certificate declaring me to be an Indo-British subject named Abdullah, by profession a doctor, and, to judge from frequent blanks in the document, not distinguished by any remarkable conformation of eyes, nose, or cheek. This paper, duly countersigned by the Zabit, or Police Magistrate, would carry me anywhere within the Egyptian frontier.

At Alexandria also I provided a few necessaries for the Pilgrimage —a change or two of clothing, a substantial leather money belt to carry my gold, a little cotton bag for silver and small change kept ready for use in the breast pocket, a zemzemiyah, or water bag of goat-skin, a huge cotton umbrella of Cairene make, brightly yellow, like an overgrown

7   In *Personal Narrative of a Pilgrimage,* Burton wrote of the magic mirror: "This invention dates from the most ancient times, and both in the East and in the West has been used by the weird brotherhood to produce the appearances of the absent and the dead, to discover treasure, to detect thieves, to cure disease, and to learn the secrets of the unknown world" (1:387n). Further details are included in "Spiritualism in Eastern Lands" (1878), reprinted in Burton, *Selected Papers on Anthropology, Travel & Exploration,* ed. N. M. Penzer (London, 1924), 184-209.

marigold, a coarse Persian rug, which acted [as] bed, table, chair, and oratory, a pea-green box with red and yellow flowers, capable of standing falls from a camel twice a day and therefore well fitted for a medicine chest, and, lastly, the only peculiar article was the shroud, without which no person sets out en route to Meccah. This *memento mori* is a piece of cotton six feet long by five broad. It is useful, for instance, when a man is dangerously sick or wounded; the caravan, of course, cannot wait, and to loiter behind is destruction. The patient, therefore, is ceremonially washed, wrapped up in his "Kafan," partly covered with sand, and left to his fate. It is hard to think of such an end without horror; the torturing thirst of a wound, the sun heating the brain to madness, and, worst of all—for they do [not] wait till death—the attacks of the jackal, the vulture, and the ravens of the wild. The shroud was duly sprinkled, as is the custom, with the Holy Water of the Zemzem Well at Meccah: it came to a bad end amongst the villainous Somal in Eastern Africa.

Equipped in a Dervish's frock, I took leave of my kind host and set out, a third-class passenger, upon a steamer facetiously known as the "Little Asthmatic." In those days the Rail had not invaded Egypt. We had an unpleasant journey up the Mahmudiyah Canal and the Nile, which is connected by it with Alexandria. The usual time is thirty hours: we took three mortal days and nights: we were nearly wrecked at the then unfinished Barrage,⁸ we saw nothing of the Pyramids but their tops, and it was with a real feeling of satisfaction that we moored alongside of the old tumble-down suburb, Bulak.

My Dervishhood was perfectly successful. I happened by chance to touch the elbow of an Anglo-Indian officer when he half privily half publicly condemned my organs of vision. And I made an acquaintance and a friend on board. The former was a shawl and cotton merchant, Miyan Khudabaksh Namdar, of Lahore, who, as the caravanserais were full of pilgrims, lodged me at his house for a fortnight. The conversations which passed between us were published in 1855 (*A Pilgrimage to El Medinah and Meccah*, Chapt. 3).⁹ They clearly pointed to the mutiny which

---

8 In *Personal Narrative of a Pilgrimage*, Burton remarked that the Barrage "was intended to act as a dam, raising the waters of the Nile and conducting them to Suez, the salt lakes, and a variety of other places, through a number of canals, which, however, have not yet been opened" (1:30n).

9 In *Personal Narrative of a Pilgrimage*, Burton does not record these conversations in detail, but writes of the inappropriateness of relaxed conversation with such a person. "Like the fox in the fable, fulsomely flattering at first, he gradually becomes easily friendly, disagreeably familiar, offensively rude" (1:37).

occurred two years afterwards, and this, together with my frankness about the Suez Canal (Chapt. 6), did not tend to make me a favourite with the effete Government of India.[10]

My friend was a Turkish trader, named Haji Wali-el-din, who still I believe lives in a village near Cairo. He was then a man about forty-five, of middle stature, with a large round head closely shaven, a bull neck, limbs sturdy as a Saxon's, a thin red beard, and handsome features beaming benevolence. A curious dry humour he had, delighting in "quizzing," but in so quiet, quaint, and solemn a way that before you knew him you could scarce divine his drift. He presently found for me rooms next to his own at the Wakalah, or Caravanserai, called Jemeliyah, in the Greek Quarter, and I tried to repay his kindness by counselling him in an unpleasant Consular suit.

When we lived under the same roof, the Haji and I became inseparable. We walked together and dined together, and spent the evening at a mosque or other place of public pastime. Sometimes we sat amongst the Dervishes, but they are a dangerous race, travelled and inquisitive. Meanwhile I continued to practise my profession—the medical—and I devoted several hours a day to study in the Azhar Mosque, sitting under the learned Shaykh Mohammed Ali Attar. The better to study the "humours," I also became a grocer-druggist, and my little shop, a mere hole in the wall, was a perfect gem of Nilotic queerness. But although I sold my wares under cost price to fair customers, my chief clients were small boys and girls, who came, halfpence in hand, to buy sugar and pepper. So one day, determining to sink the thirty shillings which my stock in trade had stood me, I locked the wooden shutter that defended my establishment and made it over to my Shaykh.

The Haji and I fasted together during the month of Ramazan: that year it fell in torrid June, and it always makes the Moslem unhealthy and unamiable. At the end, preparations were to be made for departure Meccah-wards, and the event was hastened by a convivial séance with a Bacchanalian Captain of Albanians, which made the gossips of the quarter wonder what manner of an Indian doctor had got amongst them.

I was fortunate enough, however, to hire the services of Shaykh Nur, a quiet East Indian, whose black skin made society suppose him to be

---

10 In *Personal Narrative of a Pilgrimage*, Burton wrote: "The English want a rail road, which would confine the use of Egypt to themselves. The French desire a canal that would admit the hardy cruisers of the Mediterranean into the Red Sea. The cosmopolite will hope that both projects may be carried out" (1:113).

my slave. Never suspecting my nationality till after our return from Meccah, he behaved honestly enough; but when absolved by pilgrimage from his past sins, Haji Nur began to rob me so boldly that we were compelled to part. I also made acquaintance with certain sons of the Holy Cities—seven men from El Medinah and Meccah—who, after a begging-trip to Constantinople, were returning to their homes. Having doctored them and lent them some trifling sums, I was invited by Shaykh Hamid El Samman to stay with him at El Medinah, and by the boy Mohammed El Basyuni to lodge at his mother's house in Meccah. They enabled me to collect the proper stores for the journey: these consisted of tea, coffee, loaf sugar, biscuit, oil, vinegar, tobacco, lanterns, cooking-pots, and a small bell-shaped tent costing twelve shillings. The provisions were placed in a Kafas, or hamper, of palm sticks; my drugs and dress in a Sahharah, or wooden box some three and half feet each way, covered with cowskin, and the lid fitting into the top. And finally, not wishing to travel by the vans then allotted to the overland passengers, I hired two dromedaries and their attendant Bedouins, who for the sum of ten shillings each agreed to carry me across the Desert between Cairo and Suez.

At last, after abundant trouble, all was ready. At 3 p.m. (July 1, 1853), my friend Haji Wali embraced me heartily, and so did my poor old Shaykh, who, despite his decrepitude and my objections, insisted upon accompanying me to the City Gate. I will not deny having felt a tightening of heart as their honest faces and forms faded in the distance. All the bystanders ejaculated, "Allah bless thee, Y'al Hajj (O pilgrim!), and restore thee to thy family and thy friends." We rode hard over the stretch of rock and hard clay which is now yielding to that monumental work, the Suez Canal. There was no ennui upon the road: to the traveller there is an interest in the wilderness

Where love is liberty and Nature law

unknown to Cape seas and Alpine glaciers and even the boundless prairie. I felt as if looking once more upon the face of a friend, and my two Bedouins—though the old traveller [Sir John Mandeville] described their forefathers as "folke full of all evylle condiciouns"—were excellent company. At midnight we halted for a little rest near the then Central Station, and after dark on the next evening I passed through the tumble-down gateway of Suez and found a shelter in the Wakalah Jirjis—the

George Inn. My Meccan and Midinite friends were already installed there, and the boy Mohammed El Basyuni had joined me on the road.

It was not easy to embark at Suez: in those days the greater body of pilgrims marched round the head of the Red Sea. Steamers were rare, and in the spirit of protection the Bey, or Governor, had orders to obstruct us till near the end of the season. Most Egyptian high officials sent their boats laden with pious travellers up the Nile, whence they returned freighted with corn: they naturally did their best to force upon us the delays and discomforts of what is called the Kussayr (Cosseir) line. And as those who travelled by the land route spent their money fifteen days longer in Egyptian territory than they would have done if allowed to embark at Suez, the Bey assisted them in the former and obstructed them in the latter case.

We were delayed in the George Inn four mortal days and nights amidst all the plagues of Egypt. At last we found a sambuk, or small half-decked vessel, about to start, and for seven dollars each, we took places upon the poop, the only possible part in the dreadful summer months. The "Silk El Zahab," or "Golden Thread," was probably a lineal descendant from the ships of Solomon harboured in Ezion Geber. It was about fifty tons burden, and we found ninety-seven, instead of sixty, the proper number of passengers. The farce of a quarter-deck ten feet by eight accommodated eighteen of us, and our companions were Maghribis, men from North-Western Africa—the most quarrelsome and vicious of pilgrims.

We sailed on the 6th of July, and, as in an Irish packet of the olden time, the first scene or preliminary to "shaking down" was a general fight. The Rais (Captain) naturally landed and left us to settle the matter, which ended in many a head being broken. I played my poor part in the mêlée by pushing down a heavy jar full of water upon the swarm of assailants. At last the Maghribis, failing to dislodge us from the poop, made peace, and finding that we were Sons of the Holy Cities, became as civil as their unkindly natures permitted. We spent twelve days, instead of the normal five, beating down the five hundred and fifty direct miles between Suez and Yambu.

Every two days we managed to land and stretch our limbs. The mornings and evenings were mild and balmy, the days were terrible: we felt as if a few more degrees of heat would be fatal. The celebrated coral reefs of the Red Sea, whence some derive its name, appeared like meadows of brilliant flowers resembling those of earth, only far brighter and more beautiful. The sunsets were magnificent; the zodiacal light, or after-glow, was a study, and the cold rays of the moon, falling upon a wilderness of white crag and pinnacle, suggested a wintry day in England.

At last, after slowly working up a narrow creek leading to the Yambu harbour, on July 17 we sprang into a shore-boat, and felt new life when bidding eternal adieu and sweet bad luck to the "Golden Wire" which seemed determined to wreck herself about once per diem.

Yambu, the port of El Medinah, lies S.S. West of, and a little over a 130 miles from, its city. The road is infamous—rocky, often waterless, alternately fiery and freezing, and infested with the Beni Harb, a villainous tribe of hill Bedouins. Their chief was one Saad, a brigand of the first water; he is described as a little brown man, contemptible in appearance but remarkable for courage and a ready wit, which has saved him from the poison and pistol of his enemies. Some call him the friend of the poor, and all know him as the enemy of the rich.

There was nothing to see at Yambu, where, however, we enjoyed the Hamman [a hot bath] and drinking-water, which appeared deliciously sweet after the briny supplies of Suez. By dint of abundant bargaining we hired camels at the moderate rate of three dollars each—half in ready money and the rest to be paid after arrival. I also bought a Shugduf, or rude litter carrying two, and chose the boy Mohammed as my companion. The journey is usually done in five days: we took eight and considered ourselves lucky.

On the evening of the next day (July 18) we set out with all the gravity of men putting our heads into the lion's jaws. The moon rose fair and clear as we emerged from the shadowy streets and when we launched into the Desert, the sweet, crisp air delightfully contrasted with their close, offensive atmosphere.

My companions all, as Arabs will do on such occasions, forgot to think of their precious boxes full of the plunder of Constantinople and began to sing. We travelled till three o'clock in the morning: these people insist upon setting out in the afternoon and passing the night in travelling. And the Prophet informs us that the "Calamities of Earth," meaning scorpions, serpents, and wild beasts, are least dangerous during the dark hours.

After a pleasant sleep in the wilderness, we joined for the next day's march a caravan of grain carriers, about 200 camels escorted by seven Turkish Bashi Bazouk, or Irregular Cavalry. They confirmed the report that the Bedouins were "out," and declared that Saad, the Old Man of the Mountain, had threatened to cut every throat venturing into his passes.

That night the robbers gave us a mild taste of their quality, and soon ran away. The third day [lay] over an iron land and under a sky of brass to a long straggling village called, from its ruddy base, El Hamra, the Red: it is the middle station between Yambu and El Medinah. The fourth march placed us on the Sultan's high-road leading from Meccah to the Prophet's burial-place, and we joined a company of pious persons bound on visitation. The Bedouins, hearing that we had an escort of 200 troopers, manned a gorge and would not let us advance till the armed men retired. The fifth and sixth days were forced halts at a vile place called Bir Abbas, where we could hear the distant dropping of musketry, a sign that the troops and the hillmen were settling some little dispute. Again my companions were in cold perspirations about their treasures, and they passed the most of their time in sulking and quarrelling.

About sunset on the 23rd of July, three or four caravans assembled at Bir Abbas, forming one large body for better defence against the dreaded Bedouins. We set out at 11 p.m., travelled without halting through the night, and at early dawn found ourselves in an ill-famed narrow known as Shuab el Hajj, or the Pilgrim's Pass. The boldest looked apprehensive when we approached it. Presently, from the precipitous cliff on our left, thin puffs of blue smoke rose in the sultry morning air, and instantly afterwards, the sharp cracks of the hill-men's matchlocks were echoed by the rocks on the right. A number of Bedouins could be seen swarming like hornets up the steeper slopes, carrying huge weapons and spoiling for a fight. They took up comfortable positions on the cut-throat eminence and began practising upon us from behind their breast-works of piled stones with perfect convenience to themselves. We had nothing to do but to blaze away as much powder and to veil [ourselves] in as dense a smoke as possible. The result was that we lost twelve men, besides camels and other beasts of burden. My companions seemed to consider this questionable affair a most gallant exploit.

The next night (July 24) was severe. The path lay up rocky hill and down stony vale. A tripping and stumbling dromedary had been substituted for my better animal, and the consequence may be imagined.

The sun had nearly risen before I shook off the lethargic effects of such a march. All around, men were hurrying their beasts, regardless of rough ground, and not a soul spoke a word to his neighbour. "Are there robbers in sight?" was the natural question. "No," responded the boy

View of El Medinah, taken from the Harrah (or ridge) west of the town; from *Personal Narrative of a Pilgrimage to El Medinah and Meccah* (1855). Burton was critical of contemporary depictions of Medina and Mecca. In *Personal Narrative*, he wrote: "Nothing can be more ludicrous than the views of the Holy City, as printed in our popular works. They are of the style 'bird's-eye,' and present a curious perspective. They despise distance like the Chinese,—pictorially audacious; the Harrah, or ridge in the foreground appears to be 200 yards, instead of three or four miles from the Town" (1:341n).

Mohammed. "They are walking with their eyes; they will presently sight their homes."[11]

Half an hour afterwards we came to a huge Mudarrij, or Flight of Steps, roughly cut in a long broad line of black scoriaceous basalt. Arrived at the top, we passed through a lane of dark lava with steep banks on both sides, and in a few minutes a full view of the Holy City suddenly opened upon us. It was like a vision in The Arabian Nights. We halted our camels as if by word of command. All dismounted, in imitation of the pious of old, and sat down, jaded and hungry as we were, to feast our eyes on the "Country of Date Trees," which looked so passing fair after the "Salt Stony Land." As we looked eastward the sun rose out of the horizon of blue and pink hill, the frontier of Nijd staining the spacious plain with gold and purple. The site of El Medinah is in the west-

---

11　In *Personal Narrative of a Pilgrimage,* Burton glosses this remark: "That is to say, they would use, if necessary, the dearest and noblest parts of their bodies (their eyes) to do the duty of the basest (i.e. their feet)" (1:278n).

View of El Medinah, the burial place of the Prophet. From *Personal Narrative of a Pilgrimage to El Medinah and Meccah* (1855).

ern edge of the highlands which form the plateau of Central Arabia. On the left or north was a tall, grim pile of porphyritic rock, the celebrated Mount Ohod, with a clump of verdure and a dome or two nestling at its base. Round a whitewashed fortalice founded on a rock clustered a walled city, irregularly oval, with tall minarets enclosing a conspicuous green dome. To the west and south lay a large suburb and long lines of brilliant vegetation piercing the tawny levels. I now understood the full value of a phrase in the Moslem ritual—"And when the Pilgrim's eyes shall fall upon the trees of El Medinah, let him raise his voice and bless the Prophet with the choicest of blessings."

In all the panorama before us nothing was more striking, after the desolation through which we had passed, than the gardens and orchards about the town. My companions obeyed the command with the most poetical exclamations, bidding the Prophet "live for ever whilst the west wind bloweth gently over the hills of Nijd and the lightning flasheth bright in the firmament of El Hejaz."

We then remounted and hurried through the Bab El Ambari, the gate of the Western Suburb. Crowded by relatives and friends, we passed down a broad, dusty street, pretty well supplied with ruins, into an open space called Barr El Manakhah, or "place where camels are made to kneel." Straight forward a line leads directly into the Bab el Misri, the

Egyptian gate of the city. But we turned off to the right, and after advancing a few yards we found ourselves at the entrance of our friend Shaykh Hamid's house. He had preceded us to prepare for our reception.

No delay is allowed in the Ziyarat, or Visitation of the Haram, or Holy Place, which received the mortal remains of the Arab Prophet: we were barely allowed to breakfast, to perform the religious ablution, and to change our travel-soiled garments. We then mounted asses, passed through the Egyptian, or western, gate, and suddenly came upon the mosque. It is choked up with ignoble buildings, and as we entered the Door of Mercy I was not impressed by the spectacle.

The site of the Prophet's mosque—Masjid el Nabawhi, as it is called —was originally a graveyard shaded by date trees: the first walls were of adobe, or unbaked brick, and the recently felled palm-trunks were made into pillars for the leaf-thatched roof. The present building, which is almost four centuries old, is of cut stone, forming an oblong of 420 feet by 340 feet. In the centre is a spacious uncovered area containing the "Garden of Our Lady Fatimah"—a railed plot of ground bearing a lote tree and a dozen palms. At the south-east angle of this enclosure, under a wooden roof and columns, is the "Prophet's Well," whose water is hard and brackish. Near it meets the City Academy, where in the cool mornings and evenings the young idea is taught to shout rather than to shoot.

Around the Court are four Riwaks, or Porches, not unlike the Cloisters of a monastery; they are arched to the front, backed by the wall and supported inside by pillars of different shape and material, varying from dirty plaster to fine porphyry. When I made my visitation, the northern porch was being rebuilt; it was to be called after Abd El Majid, the then reigning Sultan, and it promised to be the most splendid. The main colonnade, however, the sanctum containing all that is venerable in the building, embraces the whole length of the southern short wall, and is deeper than the other three by nearly treble the number of columns. It is also paved with handsome slabs of white marble and marquetry work, here and there covered with coarse matting and above this by unclean carpets, well worn by faithful feet.

To understand the tomb a few preliminary remarks are necessary. Mohammed, it must be remembered, died in the eleventh year of his mission and the sixty-third of his age, corresponding with anno Dom. 632. He was accustomed to say, "In whatsoever spot a Prophet departs this life, there also should he be buried." Accordingly his successor ordered the grave to be dug in the house of the young widow Ayisha, who lived close to the original mosque. After her husband's burial she occupied an adjoining room partitioned off from the tomb at which men were accustomed to pray. Another saying of the Prophet's forbade tombs to be erected in mosques; it therefore became necessary so to contrive that the revered spot should be in, and yet not in, the place of worship.

Accordingly they built a detached tower in the south-eastern corner of the mosque, and called it the Hujrah, or Chamber. It is from fifty to fifty-five feet square, with a passage all round, and it extends from floor to roof, where it is capped by the green dome which strikes the eye on approaching the city. The external material of this closet, which also serves to protect the remains from infidels and schismatics, is metal filagree painted a vivid gray green and relieved by the brightly gilt or burnished brass-work forming the long and graceful Arabic characters. On the south side, for greater honour, the railing is plated over in parts with silver, and letters of the same metal are interlaced with it.

Entering by the western Door of Safety, we paced slowly towards the tomb down a line of wall about the height of a man, and called the "Illustrious Fronting." The barrier is painted with arabesques and pierced with four small doors. There are two niches richly worked with various coloured marbles, and near them there is a pulpit, a graceful collection of slender columns, elegant tracery, and inscriptions admirably carved. Arrived at the western small door in the dwarf wall, we entered the famous spot called El Ranzah (the Garden), after a saying of Mohammed: "Between my Grave and my Pulpit is a Garden of the Gardens of Paradise." On the north and west sides it is not divided from the rest of the porch; to the south rises the dwarf wall, and eastward it is bounded by the west end of the filagree tower containing the tomb.

The "Garden" is the most elaborate part of the mosque. It is a space of about eighty feet in length tawdrily decorated to resemble vegetation: the carpets are flowered, and the pediments of the columns are cased with bright green tiles, and the shafts are adorned with gaudy and unnatural growths in arabesque. It is further disfigured by handsome branched candelabra of cut crystal, the work, I believe, of an English house. Its peculiar background, the filagree tower, looks more picturesque near than at a distance, where it suggests the idea of a gigantic birdcage. The only really fine feature of the scene is the light cast by the window of stained glass in the southern wall. Thus little can be said in praise of the Garden by day. But at night the eye, dazzled by oil lamps suspended from the roof, by huge wax candles, and by minor illuminations, whilst crowds of visitors in the brightest attire, with the richest and the noblest of the citizens, sit in congregation to hear the services, becomes far less critical.

Entering the Garden we fronted towards Meccah, prayed, recited two chapters of the Koran and gave alms to the poor in gratitude to Allah for making it our fate to visit so holy a spot. Then we repaired to the southern front of the chamber, where there are three dwarf windows, apertures half a foot square, and placed at eye's height from the ground. The westernmost is supposed to be opposite the face of Mohammed, who lies on his right side, facing, as is still the Moslem custom, the House of Allah at Meccah. The central hole is that of Abubakr, the first Caliph, whose head is just behind the Prophet's shoulder. The most eastern window is that of Omar, the second Caliph, who holds the same position with respect to Abubakr. In the same chamber, but decorously divided by a wall from the male tenants, reposes the Lady Fatimah, Mohammed's favourite daughter. Osman, the fourth Caliph, was not buried after his assassination near his predecessors, but there is a vacant space for Isa bin Maryam when he shall return.

We stood opposite these three windows, successively, beginning with the Prophet, reciting the blessings, which we were directed to pronounce "with awe and fear and love." The ritual is very complicated, and the stranger must engage a guide technically called a Muzawwir, or visitation-maker. He is always a Son of the Holy City, and Shaykh Hamid was mine. Many a piercing eye was upon me: the people probably suspected that I was an Ajami or Persian, and these heretics have often attempted to defile the tombs of the two Caliphs.

When prayers were at an end, I was allowed to look through the Prophet's window. After straining my eyes for a time, the oil lamps shedding but a dim light, I saw a narrow passage leading round the chamber. The inner wall is variously represented to be made of stone planking or unbaked brick. One sees, however, nothing but their covering, a curtain of handsome silk and cotton brocade, green, with long white letters worked into it. Upon the hangings were three inscriptions in characters of gold, informing readers that behind them lie Allah's Prophet and the two first Caliphs. The exact place of Mohammed's tomb is, moreover, distinguished by a large pearl rosary and a peculiar ornament, the celebrated Kaukab el Durri, or constellation of pearls; it is suspended breast high to the curtain. This is described to be a "brilliant star set in diamonds and pearls" placed in the dark that man's eye may be able to endure its splendours; the vulgar believe it to be a "jewel of the jewels of Paradise." To me it suggested the round glass stopper used for the humbler sort of decanter, but I thought the same of the Koh-i-Nur.

I must allude to the vulgar story of Mohammed's steel coffin suspended in mid-air between two magnets. The myth has won a world-wide reputation, yet Arabia has never heard of it. Travellers explain it in two ways. Niebuhr supposes it to have risen from the rude ground-plan drawings sold to strangers and mistaken by them for elevations [*Travels through Arabia, and other countries in the East* 1774; trans. 1792)]. Mr. William Bankes believes that the rock popularly described as hanging unsupported in the mosque of Omar at Jerusalem was confounded with the Prophet's tomb at El Medinah by Christians, who until very lately could not have seen either of these Moslem shrines [*Narrative of the life and adventures of Giovanni Finati*, trans. W. J. Bankes (1830)].

A book which I published upon the subject of my Pilgrimage gives in detail (Chapt. 16) my reason for believing that the site of Mohammed's sepulture is doubtful as that of the Holy Sepulchre at Jerusalem [*Personal Narrative of a Pilgrimage*, 1:339-41]. They are, briefly, these four. From the earliest days the shape of the Prophet's tomb has never been generally known in El Islam. The accounts of the grave given by the learned are discrepant. The guardianship of the spot was long in the hands of schismatics (the Beni Husayu). And lastly, I cannot but look upon the tale of the blinding light which surrounds the Prophet's tomb, current for ages past, and still universally believed upon the authority of the attendant eunuchs who must know its falsehood, as a priestly gloss intended to conceal a defect.

To that book also I must refer for a description of the minor holy places at El Medinah [*Personal Narrative of a Pilgrimage*, 1:398-436]. They are about fifty in number, and of these about a dozen are generally visited. The principal of these are, first, El Bakia, the Cemetery of the Saints, to the east of the city; on the Last Day some seventy thousand, others say a hundred thousand, holy men with faces like full moons shall arise from it. The second is the Apostle's Mosque at Kuba, the first temple built in El Islam. And the third is a visitation to the tomb of Mohammed's paternal uncle, Hamzah, the "Lord of Martyrs," who was slain fighting for the faith in A.D. 625.

A few observations concerning the little-known capital of the Northern Hejaz may not be unacceptable.

Medinah El Nabi, the City of the Prophet, is usually called by Moslems for brevity, El Medinah, or the City by Excellence. It lies between the twenty-fourth and twenty-fifth degree of north latitude, corresponding therefore with Central Mexico, and being high raised above the sea, it may be called a *tierra temporada.* My predecessor, Burckhardt, found the water detestable: I thought it good. The winter is long and rigorous, hence partly the fair complexion of its inhabitants, who rival in turbulence and fanaticism their brethren of Meccah.

El Medinah consists of three parts—a town, a castle, and a large suburb. The population ranges from sixteen thousand to eighteen thousand souls, whereas Meccah numbers forty-five thousand, and when I visited it the garrison consisted of a half-battalion, or four hundred men. Mohammed's last resting-place has some fifteen hundred hearths enclosed by a wall of granite and basalt in irregular layers cemented with lime. It is pierced with four gates: the Syrian, the Gate of Hospitality, the Friday, and the Egyptian. The two latter are fine massive buildings, with double towers like the old Norman portals, but painted with broad bands of red, yellow, and other flaring colours. Except the Prophet's mosque, there are few public buildings. There are only four caravanserais, and the markets are long lines of sheds, thatched with scorched and blackened palm-leaves. The streets are what they should always be in these torrid lands, deep, dark, narrow, and rarely paved; they are generally of black earth, well watered and trodden to hardness. The houses appear well built for the East, of squared stone, flat roofed, double storied, and enclosing spacious courtyards and small gardens, where water basins and trees and shrubs "cool the eyes," as the Arabs say. Latticed balconies are here universal, and the windows are mere holes in the wall, provided with broad shutters. The castle has stronger defences than the town, and inside it a tall donjon tower bears, proudly enough, the banner of the Crescent and the Star. Its whitewashed lines of wall render this fortalice a conspicuous object, and guns pointing in all directions, especially upon the town, make it appear a kind of Gibraltar to the Bedouins.

For many reasons strangers become very much attached to El Medinah and there end their lives. My servant, Shaykh Nur, opined it to be a "very heavenly city." Therefore the mass of the population is of foreign extraction.

On the 28th of August arrived the great Damascus Caravan, which sets out from Constantinople bringing the presents of the Sublime Porte. It is the main stream which absorbs all the small currents flowing at this season of general movement from Central Asia towards the Great Centre of the Islamitic world, and in 1853 it amounted to about seven thousand souls. It was anxiously expected at El Medinah for several reasons. In the first place, it brought with it a new curtain for the Prophet's Chamber, the old one being in a tattered condition; secondly, it had charge of the annual stipends and pensions of the citizens; and thirdly, many families had members returning under its escort to their homes. The popular anxiety was greatly increased by the disordered state of the country round about, and moreover the great Caravan was a day late. The Russian War had extended its excitement even into the bowels of Arabia, and to travel eastward according to my original intention was impossible.

For a day or two we were doubtful about which road the Caravan would take, the easy coast line or the difficult and dangerous Eastern or Desert Route. Presently Saad the robber shut his doors against us, and we were driven perforce to choose the worse. The distance between El Medinah and Meccah by the frontier way would be in round numbers 250 (248) miles, and in the month of September water promised to be exceedingly scarce and bad.

I lost no time in patching up my water-skins, in laying in a store of provisions, and in hiring camels. Masud El Harbi, an old Bedouin, agreed to let me have two animals for the sum of twenty dollars. My host warned me against the treachery of the wild men, with whom it is necessary to eat salt once a day.[12] Otherwise they may rob the traveller and plead that the salt is not in their stomachs.

Towards evening time on August the 30th, El Medinah became a scene of exceeding confusion in consequence of the departure of the pilgrims. About an hour after sunset all our preparations were concluded. The evening was sultry; we therefore dined outside the house. I was told to repair to the Shrine for the Ziyarat el Wida'a, or the Farewell Visitation. My decided objection to this step was that we were all to part, and where to meet again we knew not. I therefore prayed a two-prostration prayer, and facing towards the Haram recited the usual supplication. We

---

12 In *Personal Narrative of a Pilgrimage*, Burton explains: "The old idea in Europe was, that salt is a body composed of various elements, into which it cannot be resolved by human means: hence, it became the type of an indissoluble tie between individuals" (2:53n).

sat up till 2 a.m. when, having heard no signal gun, we lay down to sleep through the hot remnant of the hours of darkness. Thus was spent my last night at the City of the Prophet.

I can hardly flatter myself with the idea that this lecture has been other than the driest, and best thanks are due for the friendly attention with which it has been honoured.

The Arabs have a proverb:

The lecture is one

The dispute (upon the subject of the lecture) is one thousand.

If anyone here present would receive an explanation of what has been read I shall be most happy to answer all questions to the best of my poor ability.

Lecture 2
The Pilgrimage to Meccah

The last time I had the honour of addressing this distinguished assembly we performed the Visitation Ceremonies before the Prophet's Tomb at El Medinah. This day we will proceed to the Meccan Pilgrimage and emerge with the cognomen of Haji.

On Wednesday, the 31st of August, 1853, I embraced my good host, Shaykh Hamid, who had taken great trouble to see us properly provided for the journey. Shortly after leaving the city [El Medinah], we all halted and turned to take a last farewell. All the pilgrims dismounted and gazed long and wistfully at the venerable minarets and the Prophet's green dome—spots upon which their memories would ever dwell with a fond and yearning interest.

We hurried after the Damascus caravan, and presently fell into its wake. Our line was called the Darb el Sharki, or eastern road. It owes its existence to the piety of Zubaydah Khatun, wife of the well-known Harun el Rashid. That estimable princess dug wells, built tanks, and raised (we are told) a wall with occasional towers between Bagdad and Meccah, to guide pilgrims over the shifting sands. Few vestiges of all this labour remained in the year of grace 1853.

Striking is the appearance of the caravan dragging its slow length along

> The Golden desert glittering through
> The subtle veil of beams,

as the poet of "Palm-leaves" has it.[1] The sky is terrible in its pitiless splendours and blinding beauty, while the simoom, or wind of the wild, caresses the cheek with the flaming breath of a lion. The filmy spray of sand and the upseething of the atmosphere, the heat-reek and the dancing of the air upon the baked surface of the bright yellow soil, blending with the dazzling blue above, invests the horizon with a broad band of deep dark green, and blurs the gaunt figures of the camels, which, at a distance, appear strings of gigantic birds.

There are evidently eight degrees of pilgrims. The lowest walk, propped on heavy staves; these are the itinerant coffee-makers, sherbet

---

1   Richard Monckton Milnes (Lord Houghton), *Palm Leaves* (London, 1844), "The Tent." "The yellow desert glimmering through / The subtle veil of beams" (p. 133).

sellers, and tobacconists, country folks driving flocks of sheep and goats with infinite clamour and gesticulation, negroes from distant Africa, and crowds of paupers, some approaching the supreme hour, but therefore yearning the more to breathe their last in the Holy City. Then come the humble riders of laden camels, mules, and asses, which the Bedouin, who clings baboon-like to the hairy rump of his animal, despises, saying:

> Honourable to the rider is the riding of the horse;
> But the mule is a dishonour, and a donkey is a disgrace.

Respectable men mount dromedaries, or blood-camels, known by their small size, their fine limbs, and their large deer-like eyes: their saddles show crimson sheep-skins between tall metal pommels, and these are girthed over fine saddle-bags, whose long tassels of bright worsted hang almost to the ground. Irregular soldiers have picturesquely equipped steeds. Here and there rides some old Arab Shaykh, preceded by his varlets performing a war-dance, compared with which the bear's performance is graceful, firing their duck-guns in the air, or blowing powder into the naked legs of those before them, brandishing their bared swords, leaping frantically with parti-coloured rags floating in the wind, and tossing high their long spears. Women, children, and invalids of the poorer classes sit upon rugs or carpets spread over the large boxes that form the camel's load. Those a little better off use a Shibriyah, or short cot, fastened crosswise. The richer prefer Shugduf panniers with an awning like a miniature tent. Grandees have led horses and gorgeously painted Takhtrawan—litters like the Bangué of Brazil—borne between camels or mules with scarlet and brass trappings. The vehicle mainly regulates the pilgrim's expenses, which may vary from five pounds to as many thousands.

I will not describe the marches in detail: they much resemble those between Yambu and El Medinah. We nighted at two small villages, El Suwayrkiyah and El Sufayna, which supplied a few provisions to a caravan of 7,000-8,000 souls. For the most part it is a haggard land, a country of wild beasts and wilder men, a region whose very fountains murmur the warning words, "Drink and Away," instead of "Rest and be thankful." In other places it is a desert peopled only with echoes, an abode of death for what little there is to die in it, a waste where, to use an Arab phrase, "La Siwa Hu"—"There is none but He." Gigantic sand columns whirl over the plains, the horizon is a sea of mirage, and everywhere

Nature, flayed and scalped, discovers her skeleton to the gazer's eye.

We passed over many ridges of rough black basalt, low plains, and basins white with nitrous salt, acacia barrens where litters were torn off [the camels' backs] by the strong thorns, and domes and streets of polished rock; now we travelled down dry torrent-beds of extreme irregularity; then we wended our way along cliffs castellated as if by man's hand, and boulders and pillars of coarse-grained granite, sometimes thirty feet high. Quartz abounded, and the country may have contained gold, but here the superficial formation has long since been exhausted. In Arabia, as in the East Indies, the precious metal still lingers. At Cairo in 1854 I obtained good results by washing sand brought from the coast of the Red Sea north of Wijh. My plan for working was rendered abortive by a certain dictum now become a favourite with the governing powers in England—namely, "Gold is getting too plentiful."[2]

Few animals except vultures and ravens met the eye. Once, however, we enjoyed a grand spectacle. It was a huge yellow lion, somewhat white about the points—a sign of age—seated in a statuesque pose upon a pedestal of precipitous rock by the wayside, and gazing upon the passing spectacle as if monarch of all he surveyed. The Caravan respected the noble beast, and no one molested it. The Bedouin of Arabia has a curious custom when he happens to fall in with a lion: he makes a profound salaam, says many complimentary things, and begs his majesty not to harm a poor man with a large family. If the brute is not hungry, the wayfarer is allowed to pass on; the latter, however, is careful when returning to follow another path. "The father of roaring," he remarks, "has repented having missed a meal."

On Friday, the 9th of September, we encamped at Zaribah, two marches, or forty-seven miles, from Meccah. This being the north-eastern limit of the sanctuary, we exchanged our everyday dress for the pilgrim garb, which is known as El Ihrám, or mortification. Between the noontide and the afternoon prayers our heads were shaved, our beards and nails were trimmed, and we were made to bathe. We then donned the attire which appears to be the obsolete costume of the ancient Arabs: it consists of two cotton cloths, each six feet long by three or four feet wide, white, with narrow red stripes and fringes—in fact, that adopted in the Turkish baths of London. One of these sheets is thrown over the back

---

2 Burton remained interested in the possibility of gold discovery in the area, as indicated by his publication *The Gold-Mines of Midian and the ruined Midianite cities* (1878).

and is gathered at the right side, the arm being left exposed. The waist-cloth extends like a belt to the knee, and, being tucked in at the waist, supports itself. The head is bared to the rabid sun, and the insteps, which must also be left naked, suffer severely.

Thus equipped, we performed a prayer of two prostrations, and recited aloud the peculiar formula of pilgrimage called Talbiyat. In Arabic it is:

> Labbayk, 'Allahumma, Labbayk!
> La Sharika laka. Labbayk!
> Jun 'al Hamda wa' n' Niamata laka w' al Mulh!
> La Sharika laka. Labbayk!

which I would translate thus:

> Here I am! O Allah! here am I!
> No Partner has Thou. Here am I!
> Verily the Praise and the Grace are thine, and the kingdom!
> No Partner hast Thou. Here am I.

The directors of our conscience now bade us be good pilgrims, avoiding quarrels, abusive language, light conversation, and all immorality. We must religiously respect the Sanctuary of Meccah by sparing the trees and by avoiding to destroy animal life, excepting, however, the "five nuisances"—a crow, a kite, a rat, a scorpion, and a biting dog. We must abstain from washes and perfumes, oils, dyes, and cosmetics; we must not pare the nails nor shave, pluck or cut the hair, nor must we tie knots in our garments. We were forbidden to cover our heads with turban or umbrella, although allowed to take advantage of the shade, to ward off the sun with our hands. And for each infraction of these ordinances we were commanded to sacrifice a sheep.

The women followed our example: this alone would disprove the baseless but world-wide calumny which declares that El Islam recognises no soul in, and consequently no future for, the opposite sex. The old fathers of the Christian Church may have held such tenet, the Mohammedans never. Pilgrimesses exchange the "lisám"—that coquettish fold of thin white muslin which veils, but does not hide, the mouth—for a hideous mask of split, dried, and plaited palm-leaves pierced with bull's eyes to admit the light. This "ugly" is worn because the veil must not touch the features. The rest of the outer garment is a long sheet of white cotton, covering the head and falling to the heels. We could hardly help laughing when these queer ghostly figures first met our sight, and, to judge from the shaking of their shoulders, they were as much amused as we were.

In mid-afternoon we left Zaribah, and presently it became apparent that although we were forbidden to take the lives of others, others were not prevented from taking ours. At 5 p.m. we came upon a wide, dry torrent-bed, down which we were to travel all night. It was a cut-throat place, with a stony, precipitous buttress on the right, faced by a grim and barren slope. Opposite us the way seemed to be barred by piles of hills, crest rising above crest in the far blue distance. Day still smiled upon the upper peaks, but the lower grounds and the road were already hung with sombre shade.

A damp fell upon our spirits as we neared this "Valley Perilous." The voices of the women and children sank I remarked into deep silence, and the loud "Labbayk!" which the male pilgrims are ordered to shout whenever possible, was gradually stilled.

The cause soon became apparent. A small curl of blue smoke on the summit of the right-hand precipice suddenly caught my eye, and, simultaneously with the echoing crack of the matchlock, a dromedary in front of me, shot through the heart, rolled on the sands. The Utajbah, bravest and most lawless of the brigand tribes of the Moslem's Holy Land, were determined to boast "on such and such a night we stopped the Sultan's Caravan one whole hour in the pass."

Ensued terrible confusion. Women screamed, children cried, and men vociferated, each one striving with might and main to urge his animal beyond the place of death. But the road was narrow and half-choked with rocks and thorny shrubs; the vehicles and animals were soon jammed into a solid immovable mass, whilst at every shot a cold shudder ran through the huge body. Our guard, the irregular horsemen, about one thousand in number, pushed up and down perfectly useless, shouting to and ordering one another. The Pacha of the soldiers had his carpet spread near the precipice, and over his pipe debated with the officers about what should be done. No one seemed to whisper, "Crown the heights."

Presently two or three hundred Wahhabis—mountaineers of Tebel Shammar in North-Eastern Arabia—sprang from their barebacked camels, with their elf-locks tossing in the wind, and the flaming matches of their guns casting a lurid light over their wild features. Led by the Sherif Zayd, a brave Meccan noble, who, happily for us, was present, they swarmed up the steep, and the robbers, after receiving a few shots, retired to fire upon our rear.

Our forced halt was now exchanged for a flight, and it required much tact to guide our camels clear of danger. Whoever and whatever fell, remained on the ground; that many were lost became evident from the boxes and baggage which strewed the shingles. I had no means of ascertaining the exact number of our killed and wounded; reports were contradictory, and exaggeration was unanimous. The robbers were said to be 150 in number. Besides honour and glory, they looked forward to the loot, and to a feast of dead camel.

We then hurried down the valley in the blackness of night, between ribbed precipices, dark and angry. The torch smoke and the night fires formed a canopy, sable above and livid below, with lightning-flashes from the burning shrubs and grim crowds hurrying as if pursued by the Angel of Death. The scene would have suited M. Doré.[3]

At dawn we issued from the Perilous Pass into the Wady Laymun, or Valley of Limes. A wondrous contrast! Nothing can be more soothing to the brain than the rich green foliage of its pomegranates and other fruit trees, and from the base of the southern hills bursts a babbling stream whose

Chiare fresche e dolci acque

flow through the garden, cooling the pure air, and filling the ear with the most delicious of melodies, the gladdest sound which nature in these regions knows.

At noon we bade adieu to the Charming Valley, which, since remote times, has been a favourite resort of the Meccan citizens.

At sunset we recited the prayers suited to the occasion, straining our eyes, but all in vain, to catch sight of Meccah. About 1 a.m. I was awoken by a general excitement around me.

"Meccah! Meccah!" cried some voices. "The Sanctuary, O, the Sanctuary!" exclaimed others, and all burst into loud "Labbayk!" not infrequently broken by sobs. With a heart felt "Alhamdu lillah," I looked from my litter and saw under the chandelier of the Southern Cross the dim outlines of a large city, a shade darker than the surrounding plain.

---

3 The book illustrations of Gustave Doré (1832-83) included a treatment of Dante's *Inferno*, published in 1861.

A cool east wind met us, showing that it was raining in the Taif hills, and at times sheet lightning played around the Prophet's birthplace—a common phenomenon, which Moslems regard as the testimony of Heaven to the sanctity of the spot.

Passing through a deep cutting, we entered the northern suburb of our destination. Then we made the Shamiyah, or Syrian quarter, and finally, at 2 a.m., we found ourselves at the boy Mohammed's house. We arrived on the morning of Sunday, the eleventh of September 1853, corresponding with the sixth of Zu'l Hijjah 1269. Thus we had the whole day to spend in visiting the haram, and a quiet night before the opening of the true Pilgrim Season, which would begin on the morrow.

After a few hours of sleep and a ceremonial ablution, we donned the pilgrim garb, and with loud and long "Labbayk!" we hastened to the Bayt Ullah, or House of Allah, as the Great Temple of Meccah is called.

At the bottom of our street was the outer Bab el Salam, or Gate of Security, looking towards the east, and held to be, of all the thirty-nine, the most auspicious entrance for a first visit.

Here we descended several steps, for the level of the temple has been preserved, whilst the foundations of the city have been raised by the decay of ages. We then passed through a broad shady colonnade divided into aisles, here four, and on the other sides three, pillars deep. These cloisters are a forest of columns upwards of 550 in number, and in shape and material they are irregular as trees. The outer arches of the colonnade are ogives, and every four support a small dome shaped like a half an orange, and white with plaster: some reckon 120, others 150, and Meccan superstition declares that they cannot be counted. The rear of the cloisters rests upon an outer wall of cut stone, finished with pinnacles, or Arab battlements, and at different points in it rise seven minarets. These are tall towers much less bulky than ours, partly circular, and partly cylindrical, built at distinct epochs, and somewhat tawdrily banded with gaudy colours.

This vast colonnade surrounds a large unroofed and slightly irregular oblong, which may be compared with an exaggeration of the Palais Royal, Paris. This sanded area is 650 feet long by 525 broad, dotted with small buildings grouped round a common centre, and is crossed by 8 narrow lines of flagged pavement. Towards the middle of it, 115 paces from the northern colonnade and 88 from the southern, and based upon an irregularly oval pavement of fine close grey gneiss, or granite, rises the far-famed Kaabah, its funereal pall contrasting vividly with the sunlit walls and the yellow precipices of the city.

There it is at last, the bourne of long and weary travel, realising the plans and hopes of many and many a year! This, then, is the Kibbal, or direction towards which every Moslem has turned in prayer since the days of Mohammed, and which for long ages before the birth of Christianity was reverenced by the Patriarchs of the East.

No wonder that the scene is one of the wildest excitement! Here are worshippers clinging to the curtain and sobbing as though their hearts would break; here some poor wretch with arms thrown on high, so that his beating breast may touch the stone of the house, appears ready to faint, and there men prostrate themselves on the pavement, rubbing their foreheads against the stones, shedding floods of tears, and pouring forth frenzied ejaculations. The most careless, indeed, never contemplate it for the first time without fear and awe. There is a popular jest against new comers that in the presence of the Kaabah they generally inquire the direction of prayer, although they have all their lives been praying towards it as the early Christians fronted Jerusalem.

But we must look more critically at this celebrated shrine.

The word Kaabah means a cube, a square, a *maison carrée*. It is called Bayt Ullah (House of God) because according to the Koran it is "certainly the first temple erected for mankind." It is also known as the "Bride of Meccah," probably from the old custom of typifying the Church Visible by a young married woman—hence probably its face-veil, its covering, and its guard of eunuchs. Externally it is a low tower of fine grey granite laid in horizontal courses of irregular depth; the stones are tolerably fitted, and are not cemented. It shows no signs of decay, and indeed, in its present form, it dates only from 1627. The shape is rather a trapezoid than a square, being forty feet long by thirty-five broad and forty-five high, the flat roof having a cubit of depression from south-west to northeast, where a gold or gilt spout discharges the drainage. The foundation is a marble base two feet high, and presenting a sharp inclined plane.

All the Kaabah except the roof is covered with a Kiswatu garment called the Tea-Veil of the House. It is a pall-like hanging, the work of a certain family at Cairo, and annually renewed. The ground is dull black, and Koranic verses interwoven into it are shining black. There is a door curtain of gold thread upon red silk, and a bright band of similar material, two feet broad, runs horizontally round the Kaabah at two-thirds of its height. This covering when new is tucked up by ropes from the roof; when old it is fastened to large metal rings welded into the basement of the building. When this peculiar adjunct to the shrine is swollen and moved by the breeze, pious Moslems believe that angels are waving their wings over it.

The only entrance to the Kaabah is a narrow door of aloe wood, in the eastern side. It is now raised seven feet, and one enters it hoisted up in men's arms. In A.D. 686, when the whole building took its present shape, it was level with the external ground. The Kaabah opens gratis ten or twelve times a year, when crowds rush in and men lose their lives. Wealthy pilgrims obtain the favour by paying for it. Scrupulous Moslems do not willingly enter it, as they may never afterwards walk about bare-footed, take up fire with their fingers, and tell lies: nor is it every one that can afford such luxuries as slippers, tongs, and truth. Nothing is more simple than the interior of the building. The walls are covered with handsome red damask, flowered over with gold, tucked up beyond the pilgrim's reach. The flat roof apparently rests upon three cross-beams connecting the Eastern and Western walls and supported by three posts of carved and ornamented aloe wood.

Between the three pillars, and about nine feet from the ground, run metal bars, to which hang many lamps, said to be gold. At the northern corner there is a dwarf door; it leads into a narrow passage and to the dwarf staircase by which the servants ascend to the roof. In the south-eastern corner is a quadrant-shaped sofa, also of aloe wood, and on it sits the guardian of the shrine.

The Hajar el Aswad, or Black Stone, of which all the world talks, is fixed in the south-eastern angle outside the house, between four and five feet from the ground, the more conveniently to be kissed. It shows a black and slaggy surface, glossy and pitch-like, worn and polished by myriads of lips; its diameter is about seven inches, and it appears only in the central aperture of a gilt or gold dish. The depth to which it extends into the wall is unknown: most people say two cubits.

Believers declare, with poetry, if not with reason, that in the Day of Atast, when Allah made covenant with the souls about to animate the sons of Adam, the instrument was placed in a fragment of the lower heaven, then white as snow, now black by reason of man's sins. The ratio-nalistic infidel opines this sacred corner-stone to be a common aerolite, a remnant of the stone-worship which considered it the symbol of power presiding over universal reproduction, and inserted by Mohammed into the edifice of El Islam. This relic has fared ill; it has been stolen and broken, and has suffered other accidents.

Another remarkable part of the Kaabah is that between the door and the black stone. It is called the Multazem, or "attached to," because here the pilgrim should apply his bosom, weep bitterly, and beg pardon for his sins. In ancient times, according to some authors, it was the place for contracting solemn engagements.

The pavement which surrounds the Kaabah is about eight inches high, and the outside is marked by an oval balustrade of some score and a half of slender gilt metal pillars. Between every two of these, cross rods support oil lamps, with globes of white and green glass. Gas is much wanted at Meccah! At the north end of and separated by a space of about five feet from the building, is El Hatrim, or the "Broken," a dwarf semicircular wall, whose extremities are on a line with the sides of the Kaabah. In its concavity are two slabs of a finer stone, which cover the remains of Ismail [Ishmael], and of his mother Hajirah [Hagar]. The former, I may be allowed to remark, is regarded by Moslems as the eldest son and the legitimate successor of Abraham, in opposition to the Hebrews, who prefer the child of the free woman. It is an old dispute and not likely to be soon settled.

Besides the Kaabah, ten minor structures dot the vast quadrangle. The most important is the massive covering of the well Zemzem. The word means "the murmuring," and here the water gushed from the ground where the child Ismail was shuffling his feet in the agonies of thirst. The supply is abundant, but I found it nauseously bitter; its external application, however, when dashed like a douche over the pilgrim, causes sins to fall from his soul like dust.

On the south-east, and near the well, are the Kubbatayn, two domes crowning heavy ugly buildings, vulgarly painted with red, green, and yellow bands and used as clock room and library. Directly opposite the Kaabah door is a short ladder or staircase of carved wood, which is wheeled up to the entrance door on the rare occasions when it is opened. North of it is the inner Bab El Salam, or Gate of Security, under which pilgrims pass in their first visit to the shrine. It is a slightly built and detached arch of stone, about fifteen feet of span wide and eighteen of height, somewhat like our meaningless triumphal arches, which come from no place and go nowhere. Between this and the Kaabah stands the

Makam Ibrahim, or Station of Abraham, a small building containing the stone which supported the Friend of Allah when he was building the house. It served for a scaffold, rising and falling of itself as required, and it preserved the impressions of Abraham's feet, especially of the two big toes. Devout and wealthy pilgrims fill the cavities with water, which they rub over their eyes and faces with physical as well as spiritual refreshment. To the north of it is a fine white marble pulpit with narrow stairs leading to the preacher's post, which is surmounted by a gilt and sharply tapering steeple. Lastly, opposite the northern, the western, and the south-eastern sides of the Kaabah stand three ornamental pavilions, with light sloping roofs resting on slender pillars. From these the representatives of the three orthodox schools direct the prayers of their congregations. The Shafei, or fourth branch, collect between the corner of the well Zemzem and the Station of Abraham, whilst the heretical sects lay claim to certain mysterious and invisible places of reunion.

I must now describe what the pilgrims do.

Entering with the boy Mohammed, who acted as my mutawwif, or circuit guide, we passed through the Inner Gate of Security, uttering various religious formulas, and we recited the usual two-prostration prayer in honour of the mosque at the Shafei place of worship. We then proceeded to the Angle of the House, in which the Black Stone is set, and there recited other prayers before beginning Tawaf, or Circumambulation. The place was crowded with pilgrims, all males—women rarely appear during the hours of light. Bareheaded and barefooted they paced the giant pavement which, smooth as glass and hot as sun could make it, surrounds the Kaabah, suggesting the idea of perpetual motion. Meccans declare that at no time of the day or night is the place ever wholly deserted.

Circumambulation consists of seven Shauts, or rounds of the house, to which the left shoulder is turned, and each noted spot has its peculiar prayers. The three first courses are performed at a brisk trot, like the French *pas gymnastique*. The four latter are leisurely paced. The origin of this custom is variously accounted for: the general idea is that Mohammed directed his followers thus to show themselves strong and active to the infidels who had declared them to have been weakened by the air of El Medinah.

At the end of the Usbu or Seven Courses we fought our way through the thin-legged host of Bedouins, and kissed the Black Stone, rubbing our hands and forehead upon it. There were some other unimportant devotions, which concluded with a douche at the well Zemzem, and with a general almsgiving. The circumambulation ceremony is performed several times in the day, despite the heat. It is a positive torture.

The visit to the Kaabah, however, does not entitle a man to be called Haji. The essence of pilgrimage is to be present at the sermon pronounced by the preacher on the Holy Hill of Arafat, distant about twelve miles from and to the east of Meccah. This performed even in a state of insensibility is valid, and to die by the wayside is martyrdom, saving all the pains and penalties of the tomb.

The visit, however, must be paid on the 8th, the 9th, and the 10th of the month Zu'l Hijjah (the Lord of Pilgrimage), the last month of the Arab year. At this time there is a great throb through the framework of Moslem society from Gibraltar to Japan, and those who cannot visit the Holy City content themselves with prayers and sacrifices at home. As the Moslem computation is lunar, the epoch retrocedes through the seasons in thirty-three years. When I visited Meccah, the rites began on September 12th and ended on September 14th, 1853. In 1862, the opening day was June 8th; the closing, June 10th.

My hearers will observe that the modern Pilgrimage ceremonies of the Moslem are evidently a commemoration of Abraham and his descendants. The practices of the Father of the Faithful when he issued from the land of Chaldea seem to have formed a religious standard in the mind of the Arab law-giver, who preferred Abraham before all the other prophets, himself alone excepted.

The day after our arrival at Meccah was the Yaum El Tarwiyah, the Day of Carrying Water, the first of the three which compose the pilgrimage season proper. From the earliest dawn the road was densely thronged with white-robed votaries, some walked, others mounted, and all shouting "Labbayk!" with all their might. As usual the scene was one of strange contrasts. Turkish dignitaries on fine horses, Bedouins bestriding swift dromedaries, the most uninteresting soldiery, and the most picturesque beggars. Before nightfall I saw no less than five exhausted and emaciated devotees give up the ghost and become "martyrs."

The first object of interest was on the left-hand side of the road. This was a high conical hill, known in books as Jabal Hira or Hara but now called Jabal Nur, or Mountain of Light, because there Mohammed's mind was first illuminated. The Cave of Revelation is still shown. It looks upon a wild scene. Eastward and Southward the vision is limited by abrupt hills. In the other directions there is a dreary landscape, with here and there a stunted acacia or a clump of brushwood growing on rough ground, where stony glens and valleys of white sand, most of them water-courses after the rare rains, separate black, grey, and yellow rocks.

Passing over El Akabah, the Steeps, an important spot in classical Arab history, we entered Muna, a hot hollow three or four miles from the barren valley of Meccah. It is a long, narrow, straggling village of mud and stone houses, single storied and double storied, built in the common Arab style. We were fated to see it again. At noon we passed Muzdalifah, or the Approacher, known to El Islam as the Minaret without the Mosque, and thus distinguished from a neighbouring building, the Mosque without the Minaret. There is something peculiarly impressive in the tall, solitary tower springing from the desolate valley of gravel. No wonder that the old Arab conquerors loved to give the high-sounding name of this oratory to distant points in their extensive empire!

Here, as we halted for the noon prayer appeared the Damascus caravan in all its glory. The "mahmil," or litter, sent by the Sultan to represent his presence, no longer a framework as on the line of march, now flashed in the sun all gold and green, and the huge white camel seemed to carry it with pride. Around the moving host of peaceful pilgrims hovered a crowd of mounted Bedouins armed to the teeth. These people often visit Arafat for blood revenge; nothing can be more sacrilegious than murder at such a season, but they find the enemy unprepared. As their draperies floated in the wind and their faces were swathed and veiled with their head-kerchiefs, it is not always easy to distinguish the sex of the wild beings that hurry past at speed. The women are as unscrupulous, and many of them are seen emulating the men in reckless riding, and striking with their sticks at every animal in their way.

Presently, after safely threading the gorge called [the Pass] of the Two Rugged Hills, and celebrated for accidents, we passed between the "Two Signs"—whitewashed pillars, or, rather tall thin walls surmounted with pinnacles. They mark the limits of the Arafat Plain, the "Standing-Ground," as it is called. Here in sight of the Holy Hill Arafat, standing boldly out from the fair blue sky, and backed by the azure peaks of Taif, all the pilgrim host raised loud shouts of "Labbayk!" The noise was that of a storm.

We then sought our quarters in the town of tents scattered over two or three miles of plain at the southern foot of the Holy Hill, and there we passed a turbulent night of prayer.

Mount Arafat during the pilgrimage. From *Personal Narrative of a Pilgrimage to El-Medinah and Meccah* (1855).

I estimated the total number of devotees to be 50,000; usually it may amount to 80,000. The Arabs, however, believe that the total of those "standing on Arafat" cannot be counted, and that if less than 600,000 human beings are gathered together, the angels descend and make up the sum. Even in A.D. 1853 my Moslem friends declared that 150,000 immortals were present in mortal shape.

The Mount of Mercy, which is also called Jabal Ilál, or Mount of Wrestling in Prayer, is physically considered a mass of coarse granite, split into large blocks and thinly covered with a coat of withered thorns. It rises abruptly to a height of 180 to 200 feet from the gravelly flat, and it is separated by a sandy vale from the last spurs of the Taif hills. The dwarf wall encircling it gives the barren eminence a somewhat artificial look, which is not diminished by the broad flight of steps winding up the southern face, and by the large stuccoed platform near the summit, where the preacher delivers the "Sermon of the Standing."

Arafat means "Recognition," and owes its name and honours to a well-known legend. When our First Parents were expelled from Paradise, which, according to Moslems, is in the lowest of the Seven Heavens, Adam descended at Ceylon, Eve upon Arafat. The former, seeking his wife, began a journey to which Earth owes its present mottled appearance. Wherever he placed his foot a town arose in the fulness of time; between the strides all has remained country. Wandering for many years he came to the Mountain of Mercy, where our common mother was continually calling upon his name, and their recognizing each other gave the place its name. Upon the hill-top, Adam, instructed by the Archangel Gabriel, erected a prayer-station, and in its neighbourhood the pair abode until death.

My hearers may be pleased to know that Adam's grave is shown at Muna, the village through which we passed to day. The mosque covering his remains is called El Khayf; his head is at one end of the long wall, his feet are at the other, and the dome covers his middle. Our first father's forehead, we are told, originally brushed the skies, but this stature being found inconvenient, it was dwarfed to 150 feet. Eve, again, is buried near the port of Meccah—Jeddah, which means the "grandmother." She is supposed to lie, like a Moslemah, fronting the Kaabah, with her head southwards, her feet to the north, and her right cheek resting on her right hand. Whitewashed and conspicuous to the voyager from afar is the dome opening to the west, and covering a square stone fancifully carved to represent her middle. Two low parallel walls about eighteen feet apart define the mortal remains of our mother, who, as she measured 120 paces from head to waist and 80 from waist to heel, must have presented in life a very peculiar appearance. The archaeologist remembers that the great idol of Jeddah in the age of the Arab litholatry was a "long stone."

The next day, the 9th of the month Zu'l Hijjah, is known as Yaum Arafat, the Day of Arafat. After ablution and prayer, we visited sundry interesting places on the Mount of Mercy, and we breakfasted late and copiously, as we could not eat again before nightfall. Even at dawn the rocky hill was crowded with pilgrims, principally Bedouins and wild men, who had secured favourable places for hearing the discourse. From noon onwards the hum and murmur of the multitude waxed louder, people swarmed here and there, guns fired, and horsemen and camel-men rushed about in all directions. A discharge of cannon about 3 p.m. announced that the ceremony of "Wukuf," or Standing on the Holy Hill, was about to commence.

The procession was headed by the retinue of the Sherif, or Prince of Meccah, the Pope of El Islam. A way for him was cleared through the dense mob of spectators by a cloud of macebearers and by horsemen of the desert carrying long bamboo spears tufted with black ostrich feathers.

These were followed by led horses, the proudest blood of Arabia, and by a stalwart band of negro matchlock men. Five red and green flags immediately preceded the Prince, who, habited in plain pilgrim garb, rode a fine mule. The only sign of his rank was a fine green silk and gold embroidered umbrella, held over his head by one of his slaves. He was followed by his family and courtiers, and the rear was brought up by a troop of Bedouins on horses and dromedaries. The picturesque background of this scene was the granite hill, covered, wherever foot could be planted, with half-naked devotees, crying "Labbayk!" at the top of their voices, and violently waving the skirts of their gleaming garments. As it is not necessary to stand literally upon Arafat we contented ourselves with sighting from afar the preacher sitting, after the manner of Mohammed, on his camel and delivering the sermon.

Slowly the *cortège* wound its way towards the Mount of Mercy. Exactly at afternoon prayer-time, the two mahmil, or ornamental litters, of Damascus and Cairo take their station side by side on a platform in the lower part of the hill. A little above them stood the Prince of Meccah, within hearing of the Priest. The pilgrims crowded around them. The loud cries were stilled, and the waving of white robes ceased.

Then the Preacher began the "Sermon of the Mount," which teaches devotees the duties of the season. At first it was spoken without interruption: Then loud "Amin" and volleys of "Labbayk" exploded at certain intervals. At last the breeze came laden with a purgatorial chorus of sobs, cries, and shrieks. Even the Meccans, who, like the Sons of other Holy Cities *rarò sanctificantur* thought proper to appear affected, and those unable to squeeze out a tear buried their faces in the corners of their pilgrim cloths.

The sermon lasted about three hours, and when sunset was near, the preacher gave the Israf, or permission to depart. Then began that risky part of the ceremony known as the "Hurrying from Arafat." The pilgrims all rushed down the Mount of Mercy with cries like trumpet blasts, and took the road to Muna. Every man urged his beast to the utmost over the plain, which bristled with pegs, and was strewed with struck tents. Pedestrians were trampled, litters were crushed, and camels were thrown; here a woman, there a child, was lost, whilst night coming on without twilight added to the chaotic confusion of the scene. At the Pass of the Two Rugged Hills, where all the currents converged, was the crisis, after which progress was easier. We spent, however, at least three hours in reaching Mugdalifah, and there we resolved to sleep. The minaret was brilliantly illuminated, but my companions apparently thought more of rest and supper than of prayer. The night was by no means peaceful or silent. Lines of laden beasts passed us every ten minutes, devotees guarding their boxes from plunderers gave loud tokens of being wide awake, and the shouting of travellers continued till near dawn.

The 10th of Zu'l Hijjah, following the sermon, is called Yaum Nahr, the Day of Camel Killing, or Eed El Kurban, the Festival of the Sacrifice, the Kurban Bairam of the Turks. It is the most solemn of the year, and it holds amongst Moslems the rank which Christmas Day claims from Christendom.

We awoke at daybreak, and exchanged with all around us the compliments of the season—"Eed Kum mubarak"—"May your festival be auspicious." Then each man gathered for himself seven jamrah (bits of granite the size of a small bean), washed them "in seven waters," and then proceeded to the western end of the long street which forms the village of Muna. Here is the place called the Great Devil, to distinguish it from two others, the Middle Devil and the First Devil, or the easternmost. The outward and visible signs are nothing but short buttresses of whitewashed masonry placed against a rough wall in the main thoroughfare. Some derive the rite from the days of Adam, who put to flight the Evil One by pelting him, as Martin Luther did with his inkstand. Others opine that the ceremony is performed in imitation of Abraham, who, meeting Sathanas at Muna, and being tempted to disobedience in the matter of sacrificing his son, was commanded by Allah to drive him away with stones. Pilgrims approach if possible within five paces of the pillar, and throw at it successively seven pebbles, holding each one between the thumb and forefinger of the right hand, either extended, or shooting as a boy does a marble. At every cast they exclaim: "In the name of Allah, and Allah is Almighty! In hatred to the Fiend and to his shame I do this!" It is one of the local miracles that all the pebbles thus flung return by spiritual agency to whence they came.

As Satan was malicious enough to appear in a rugged lane hardly forty feet broad, the place was rendered dangerous by the crowd. On one side stood the Devil's buttress and wall, bristling with a *chevaux de frise* of wild men and boys. Opposite it was a row of temporary booths tenanted by barbers, and the space between swarmed with pilgrims, all trying to

Stoning the "Great Devil." From *Personal Narrative of a Pilgrimage to El-Medinah and Meccah* (1855).

get at the enemy of mankind. A monkey might have run over the heads of the mob. Amongst them were horsemen flogging their steeds, Bedouins urging frightened camels, and running footmen opening paths for the grandees, their masters, by assault and battery. We congratulated each other, the boy Mohammed and I, when we escaped with trifling hurts. Some Moslem travellers assert, by way of miracle, that no man is ever killed during the ceremony of Rajm, or lapidation. Several Meccans, however, assured me that fatal accidents are by no means rare.

After throwing the seven pebbles, we doffed our pilgrim garb, and returned to Ihlal, or the normal attire. The barber placed us upon an earthen bench in the open shop, shaved our heads, trimmed our beards, and pared our nails, causing us to repeat after him: "I purpose throwing off my ceremonial attire, according to the practice of the Prophet—whom may Allah bless and preserve! O Allah, grant to me for every hair a light, a purity, and a generous reward! In the name of Allah, and Allah is Almighty!" The barber then addressed me: "Naiman"—"Pleasure to thee!"—and I responded: "Allah, give thee pleasure!" Now we could at once use cloths to cover our heads, and slippers to defend our feet from fiery sun and hot soil, and we might safely twirl our mustachios and stroke our beards—placid enjoyments of which we had been deprived by the ceremonial law.

The day ended with the sacrifice of an animal to commemorate the substitution of a ram for Ishmael, the father of the later Arabs. The place of the original offering is in the Muna Valley, and it is still visited by pilgrims. None but the Prince, the Pacha, and high dignitaries slaughter camels. These beasts are killed by thrusting a knife into the interval between the throat and the breast, the muscles of the windpipe being too thick and hard to cut; their flesh is lawful to the Arabs, but not to the Hebrews. Oxen, sheep, and goats are made to face the Kaabah, and their throats are cut, the sacrificer ejaculating: "In the name of Allah! Allah is Almighty!" It is meritorious to give away the victim without eating any part of it, and thus crowds of poor pilgrims are enabled to regale themselves.

There is a terrible want of cleanliness in this sacrifice. Thousands of animals are cut up and left unburied in this "Devil's Punchbowl." I leave the rest to the hearer's imagination. Pilgrims generally pass in the Muna Valley the Days of Flesh-drying—namely, the 11th, the 12th, and the 13th of the month Zu'l Hijjah—and on the two former the Great, the Middle, and the Little Satan are again pelted. The standing miracles of the place are that beasts and birds cannot prey there, nor can flies settle upon provisions exposed in the markets. But animals are frightened away by the bustling crowds, and flies are found in myriads. The revolting scene, aided by a shade temperature of 120° Fahr., has more than once caused a desolating pestilence at Meccah. The cholera of 1865 has been traced back to it; in fine, the safety of Europe demands the reformation of this filthy slaughter-house.

The pilgrimage rites over, we returned to Meccah for a short sojourn. Visitors are advised, and wisely, not to linger long in the Holy City after the conclusion of the ceremonies. Use soon spoils the marvels, and, after the greater excitements, all becomes flat, stale, and unprofitable. The rite called Umrah, or the "Little Pilgrimage," and the running between Mounts Safa and Marwah, in imitation of Hagar seeking her child, remain to be performed. And there are many spots of minor sanctity to be visited, such as the Jannat El Maala, or Cemetery of the Saints, the mosque where the genii paid fealty to the Prophet, the house where Mohammed was born, that in which he lived with his first wife, Khadijah, and in which his daughter Fatimah and his grandsons Hasan and Hussayn saw the light, the place where the stone gave the founder of El Islam god-speed, and about a dozen others. Men, however, either neglect them or visit them cursorily, and think of little now beyond returning home.

I must briefly sketch the Holy City before we bid it a final and a willing adieu.

Meccah, also called Beccah, the words being synonymous, signifies according to some a "place of great concourse," is built between 21° and 22° of N. Lat. and in 39° E. Long. (Greenwich).[4] It is therefore more decidedly tropical than El Medinah, and the parallel corresponds with that of Cuba. The origin of the Bayt Ullah is lost in the glooms of time, but Meccah as it now stands is a comparatively modern place, built in A.D. 450 by Kusayr the Kuraysh. It is a city colligated together like Jerusalem and Rome. The site is a winding valley in the midst of many little hills; the effect is that it offers no general *coup d'oeil*. Thus the views of Meccah known to Europe are not more like Meccah than like Cairo or Bombay.

The utmost length of the Holy City is two miles and a half from the Mab'dah, or northern suburb, to the southern mound called Jiyad. The extreme breadth may be three-quarters between the Abu Kubays hill on the east and the Kaykaan, or Kuwaykaan, eminence on the west. The mass of houses clusters at the western base of Abu Kubays. The mounts called Safa and Marwah extend from Abu Kubays to Kaykaan, and are about 780 cubits apart. The Great Temple is near the centre of the city, as the Kaabah is near the middle of the Temple. Upon Jabal Jiyad the Greater there is a fort held by Turkish soldiery; it seems to have no great strength. In olden time Meccah had walls and gates; now there are none.

The ground in and about the Holy City is sandy and barren, the hills are rocky and desert. Meat, vegetables, and fruit must be brought from

---

4   Burton provides the following footnote at this point in the holograph. "Both latitudes and longitudes are disputed points, as the following table shows. The Arabs, it must be remembered, placed the first meridian at the Fortunate Islands:

		latitude	longitude	
The Atwal makes the		21°40',		67°13'
Kanun	"	" 21°20'	"	67° 0'
Ibu Said	"	" 21°31'	"	67°31'
Rasen	"	" 21° 0'	"	67° 0'
Khúshyar	"	" 21°40'	"	67°10'
Masr el Din	"	" 21°40'	"	77°10'
D'Anville	"	" 22° 0'	"	77°10'
Niebuhr	"	" 21°30'	"	77°10'

Humboldt, therefore, is hardly right to say: 'Le erreur est que le Mecque parassait déjà aux Arabes de 19° trop a l'est' (*Correspondence*, p. 459)."

the Eastern Highlands and grain must be imported via Jeddah, the port, distant forty-five miles. The climate is exceedingly hot and rarely tempered by the sea breeze. I never suffered so much from temperature as during my fortnight at Meccah.

The capital of the Hejaz, which is about double the size of El Medinah, has all the conveniences of a city. The streets are narrow, deep, and well watered. The houses are durable and well built of brick mixed with granite and sandstone, quarried in the neighbouring hills. Some of them are five stories high, and more like fortresses than dwelling-places. The lime, however, is bad, and after heavy rain, sometimes ten days in the year, those of inferior structure fall in ruins. None but the best have open-work of brick and courses of coloured stone. The roofs are made flat to serve for sleeping-places, the interiors are sombre to keep out the heat; they have jutting upper stories, as in the old towns of Brazil, and huge latticed hanging balconies—the maswrabujah of Cairo, here called shamiyah—project picturesquely into the streets and the small squares in which the city abounds.

The population is guessed at 45,000 souls. The citizens appeared to me more civilised and more vicious than those of El Medinah, and their habit of travel makes them a worldly-wise and God-forgetting and Mammonist sort of folk. "Circumambulate and run between Mount Safa and Marwah and do the seven deadly sins," is a satire popularly levelled against them. Their redeeming qualities are courage, *bonhomie*, manners at once manly and suave, a fiery sense of honour, strong family affections, and a near approach to what we call patriotism. The dark half of the picture is pride, bigotry, irreligion, greed of gain, debauchery, and prodigal ostentation.

Unlike his brother of El Medinah, the Meccan is a swarthy man. He is recognised throughout the East by three parallel gashes down each cheek, from the exterior angles of the eyes to the corners of the mouth. These "mashali," as they call them, are clean contrary to the commands of El Islam. The people excuse the practice by saying that it preserves their children from being kidnapped, and it is performed the fortieth day after birth.

The last pilgrimage ceremony performed at Meccah is the Tawaf el Widaa, or Circumambulation of Farewell, a solemn occasion. The devotee walks round the House of Allah, he drinks the water of the Zemzem well, he kisses the threshold of the door, and he stands for some time with his face and bosom pressed against the multazem wall, clinging to the curtain, reciting religious formula, blessing the Prophet, weeping if possible, but at least groaning. He then leaves the Temple, backing out of it with many salutations till he reaches the Gate of Farewell, when, with a parting glance at the Kaabah, he turns his face towards home.

I need not weary you with describing—how, accompanied by the boy Mohammed, I reached Jeddah on the Red Sea, how my countrymen refused for a time to believe me, and how I parted sadly with my Moslem friends. My peregrinations ended for a time, and, worn out with the fatal fiery heat, I steamed out of Jeddah on the 26th of September in the little "Dwarka," and on the 3rd of October 1853, after six months' absence from England, I found myself safely anchored in Suez Harbour.

Remains to me now only to thank you for your kind and patient attention and to say that if at any period of my sojourn you should wish to hear of my wanderings in other lands, to the Sources of the Nile for instance, amongst the Mormons, or to the Court of Dahome, you will ever find me ready to pass another pleasant hour in relating to you what I know of them.

Lecture 3
First Footsteps in Eastern Africa
Introduction

Following his pilgrimages to Medina and Mecca, Burton turned his attention to Africa. In a letter of 17 November 1853 to Dr. Norton Shaw, secretary of the Royal Geographical Society, he remarked that he would have been content to have traveled further in Arabia, but he felt that more remained to be discovered in Africa. "My wish," he wrote, "is to attack (scientifically) Zanzibar and if I can only get pay from Govt. for a few good men to accompany me (one to survey, another for physic and botany) I doubt not of our grand success."[1] Burton's first expedition to Africa was, however, to undergo a number of modifications, and Burton was subsequently to describe his intentions in different ways at different times. In his most extended account, in *First Footsteps in East Africa* (London, 1856), he indicated that he initially planned "to penetrate via Harar and Gananah to Zanzibar" (p. xix). The directors of the East India Company granted him a year's leave to accomplish this exploration, and the Royal Geographical Society provided support.

Accompanying Burton on the expedition were Lieutenants G. E. Herne, William Stroyan, and John Hanning Speke. In *First Footsteps in East Africa*, Burton described Herne as "an officer skilful in surveying, photographing, and mechanics," and Stroyan as "distinguished by his surveys of the coast of Western India, in Sindh, and on the Panjab rivers" (p. xxiii). Speke was perhaps not so easy to describe, and Burton noted that he permitted him to join the expedition as a favor. Speke, he remarked, was essentially interested in shooting game and needed the support of an expeditionary force.

The opposition of the British authorities at Aden subsequently resulted in Burton's setting out for Harar alone, with the intention of showing that such an expedition was possible. Meanwhile, Speke was given the task of tracing the Wady Nogal river, and Herne and Stroyan were to remain on the Somali coast at Berbera in case it became necessary to rescue Burton. This precaution was probably judicious. Unlike the shrines

---

1 Subsequent references to this correspondence (in the archives of the Royal Geographical Society) are included in the text.

at Medina and Mecca, Harar had not previously been visited by English explorers, and both the route and the destination were hazardous. In setting out from Zayla on 27 November 1854 with a reduced exploration party, Burton was displaying a characteristic bravado.

It is in his lecture that Burton indicated most clearly that he contemplated from the inception of the expedition a more ambitious exploration which would aim to discover the source of the White Nile. In his letter to Shaw of 17 November 1853, he had remarked on reports of explorations by the missionary Dr. J. L. Krapf, "discoveries about sources of the White Nile, Killamanjaro, and Mts of the moon which remind one of a de Lunatico." "I have not seen him," Burton continued, "but don't intend to miss the spectacle, especially to pump what really has been done and what remains to be done." Following his expedition to Harar, he felt even more determined to search for the source of the Nile and again indicated this to Shaw. "My success at Harar has emboldened me," he wrote on 25 February 1855 from Aden, "and I have applied for a 2nd years leave. . . . I want to settle the question of Krapf and 'eternal snows.' There is little doubt of the White Nile being thereabouts."

Unfortunately, following a regrouping at Berbera, the enterprise ended in disarray when it was attacked by Somalis. It has been persuasively argued that this catastrophic conclusion to the expedition was to have a lasting effect on Burton's career as an explorer.[2] Moreover, the expedition was momentous in that it initiated the relationship of Burton and Speke. Indeed, their subsequent hostility is foreshadowed by Speke's annoyance when Burton edited and published his journal as an appendix to *First Footsteps in East Africa*. Piqued by this, Speke retrieved this account and presented it fully within *What Led to the Discovery of the Source of the Nile* (1864).

Burton's title, *First Footsteps in East Africa*, was pointed, since it served to indicate his more ambitious intention. Even more pointedly, the manuscript of the lecture suggests that he originally planned to entitle the lecture "What led to the Discovery of the Sources of the Nile," though he appears also to have crossed out this title. In *The Nile Basin* (London, 1864), Burton had earlier criticized Speke's title—"when nearly

---

2 See Gordon Waterfield, ed., *First Footsteps in East Africa, by Sir Richard Burton* (New York, 1966), Preface and Introduction, ix, 41.

all Europe had made up its mind that 'Non-Discovery' would be the more fitting term, and that 'Sources,' not 'Source,' would be the proper number" (p. 23). In his lecture, there are also references to "Nile Sources," both at the opening and close. However, these references are not presented polemically, and this is an avoidance of the contentious which is quite uncharacteristic of Burton. Even more uncharacteristic is the conclusion of the lecture, when Burton comes close to admitting that he may have been responsible for the catastrophe which finally struck the expedition.

Lecture 3
First Footsteps in Eastern Africa

In my first two Lectures, I had the high honour of telling you the story of a certain Pilgrimage to Meccah. For this evening I venture to propose my "First Footsteps in Eastern Africa"—a journey which led directly to the Discovery of the Nile Sources—as far as they are now discovered.

Before plunging into the hot depths of the Dark Continent, we will briefly survey its principal features.

Africa according to geography books is "4330 nautical miles from Cape Agulhas, East of the Cape of Good Hope, to Cape Bianco, near Bizerta, its Northern most extremity. Its breadth is 4000 between C. Guardafui on the Indian Ocean and C. Verde on the Atlantic. From the irregularity of its figure"—which is painfully regular—"its area has only 12 millions of Square Miles." (Mrs. [Mary] Somerville [*Physical Geography* (London, 1848)], Chapt. 7).

Thus far the popular writer, to whom only data and facts are wanting. But in truth the area and the population of Africa are equally unknown. Of the outline we have long formed accurate ideas. The Northern half is an irregular square forming about the Equator a base for a triangle pointing South. We still await an explanation of "the reason why," but this is the normal form of great Peninsulas: for instance, Corea, Siam, Greenland, the Indian Dakhan (Deccan) and notably South America of whose resemblance to Africa I have something to say. Prof. Ritter describes negroland as a trunk without branches, whereas Asia ramifies on three sides and Europe almost everywhere.[1] Mr. Missionary Rebmann remarks that the "massive monotonous continent wears the appearance of a huge monster-slave, bent down by his burden, and looking despondingly towards America."[2] But I do not see why his face

---

1   In *Comparative Geography* (Edinburgh and London, 1865), Carl Ritter remarked on "the almost star-shaped figure which the combined body of great peninsulas assume," and he found in this shape "the working out of some great design" (p. 50). In addition, he declared: "Asia is . . . a trunk with profuse richness of articulation. Africa is a trunk without articulation—a mere compact continental mass" (pp. 193-94). He related the especially "complex articulation" of Europe to its rich and varied life.

2   Reverend John Rebmann embarked for Zanzibar on 21 January 1846, where he joined Dr. Ludwig Krapf as a missionary. Extracts from Rebmann's letters were printed in *Church Missionary Record* in subsequent years, but I have not discovered Burton's quotation there.

should wear that expression: America has been the negro's best friend—
to him the saddest view in the world must be the way home.

North Africa was not unknown to the ancients. I have supported
from modern evidence that about B.C. 600, Hanno the Carthaginian visited the Cameroon mountains in N. Lat. 4° and near there captured the
first Gorillas.[3] The Roman legions crossed the Sahil or Seaboard, the
Bilad el Jerid or Datelands, the Sahara or Great Desert, and probably
extended to Yoruba, the Nago Country in N. Lat. 6°. They did not ignore
Lake Chad, the recipient of the Shary River and of the Yevu which is
compared by Dr Barth [*Travels and Discoveries in North and Central Africa
. . . 1849-55* (1857)] to the Nile in flood. On the Eastern Coast the Egyptian and Arab, the Persian and Baloch, the Greek and Roman produced a
mixed race which still remains. Doubtless the continent was often cir-
cumnavigated and according to Walckenaer [*Abrégé de geographique
Moderne* (1811)] the Cape of Good Hope was named before its official discovery. However that may be, the exploit of Vasco da Gama in 1498
taught the truth respecting the Southern contour, and the Eastern and
Western sweep of the Ptolemean maps disappeared for ever.

The outline duly settled, fancy-geographers proceeded to dispose of
the interior, and they so turned the public mind that "desert as Central
Africa" is still a proverb. They never thought of comparing it with South
America, or of asking themselves how an Equatorial Region with the
maximum of perpendicular sun and almost ceaseless rain can possibly
be a sandy waste. But finding a desert in the North and a desert in the
South they unthinkingly connected the two.

The ancients, I have said, were acquainted with the Sahara which
subtends the Northern Seaboard—a wilderness only because it contains
no running water and few wells. They therefore supposed that the
regions to the South consisted of elevated sandy plains, into which rivers
ran and were lost. The early explorers from the South—Portuguese,
Dutch, and English—passed through the Karru which in the Hottentot
tongue means "hard" (ground), and entered the sterile country of the
Balakahari. This is a solid level block of granite, thinly clothed with
earth, with an area of some 9000 square miles raised from 2000 to 3600
feet above sea-level, and extending to S. Lat 20°.

---

3   Burton's account of his quest for gorillas, based on an expedition of 1862,
    appeared in *Two Trips to Gorilla Land and the Cataracts of the Congo* (London,
    1876). See especially chapter 11, "Mr, Mrs, and Master Gorilla," 238-52.

Reasoning on these data, the *vox populi* filled up Central Africa with a vast sandy plateau. The philosopher Lacepède supplied the interior with lofty mountains ("Mémoire Sur le grand Plateau de l'intérieur de l'Afrique," *Annales du Musée d'Histoire Naturelle* VI. 284). Prof. Ritter in 1830 elaborated an ingenious but erroneous system of "gradines"—steps or terraces, successively culminating to the Centre: he also made all Africa a highland (hoch-land) from the Cape to N. Lat. 10°, and the rest a flat country (flach-land). Thus he artistically reversed fact.[4]

Actual exploration changed all that. Early in the present century travellers reached Lake Chad in N. Lat. 14° and found it the threshold of a region where bestial and even human life can hardly contend against the luxuriance of the vegetable world. Drs. Ruppel [*Reise in Abyssinien and Atlas* (Frankfurt, 1838-40)] and Beke proved that the summit-line of the Continent was not in the interior but near the coast. In August 1849, Dr Livingstone, after a month's journey over 300 miles of desert, reached Lake Ngami in S. Lat. 20° 20' 0". This water, from 50 to 70 miles long, and two thousand feet above Sea-level, is a Southern Counterpart of Lake Chad, and between the two a depth of 34° or 200 miles range the limits of the heavy tropical rains.

Already in 1802 certain Pombeiros in trading blacks had crossed the African Continent from Luanda to the mouth of the Zambezi; their accounts of its stupendous fertility attracted little attention. They were followed by Dr Livingstone, who reconnoitered the water system between S. Lat. 10° and 20° and between the Atlantic and the Indian Oceans. He found it a land oppressed by vegetation, except where the rains are stopped by mountain ranges; a net-work of gigantic streams; of lakes or "fever-ponds"; of primeval forests; of park-like meadows; of hills, tree-clad from foot to summit; of vast swamps and of dreary starving lands where no man dwells.

Thus we came to a true knowledge of Inner Africa, whose main features have now been sketched, whilst little but detail remains to be filled in. The shape is a raised trough, an elevated basin, originally lacustrine, composed of limestones, sandstones, breccias, calcareous tufas and similar Neptunian deposits. The heavy rains gather in huge lakes, and these again send forth immense rivers. The main streams drain to the Sea

---

4   In *Comparative Geography,* Carl Ritter admitted his error of "more than thirty years ago" on "the plateau systems of central Asia and Africa" (p. 89). However, he retained a keen interest in the "transition terraces" between highland and lowland (p. 186).

through gaps and fissures in the fringe of igneous and granitic forma-
tions, which flank the Central hollow to the East and West, and which
may be called the rim of the basin. Through these walls which rarely
exceed a height of 5000 feet above sea-level, the Nile bursts to the North,
the Zambezi to the East, and the Niger and the Congo to the West.

And here I may briefly remark how much Africa resembles S.
America, not only in its triangular shape and austral projection and sea-
fringing Sierras, but also in the disposition of the interior. Both are
watery plateaus of less elevation than the mountain ranges which flank
them. But the New World, of happier destiny, is richly supplied with
ports and harbours, whilst its superficies is only 399 to l of coast line. In
Africa the ratio is 530 to 1 (Europe, on the other hand, shows 164 to 1),
and the unbroken inhospitable contour has for long ages doomed her,
despite all the efforts of Europe and Asia, to torpid barbarism. In the latter also the equatorial mean temperature is 85° 10l F. whilst happier Asia
shows 82° 94 F. and happiest America 80° 96 F. It is therefore no wonder
that the Angel of Death broods over the dark Continent, and that it has
unanimously been called the White Man's Grave.

I now proceed to my narrative.

Returning to Bombay early in 1854, I volunteered to explore the Land
of the Somal, the eastern horn of Africa, extending from Cape Guardafui
(N. Lat. 12°) to near the Equator. For long years naval officers had coast-
ed along it; many of our ships had been lost there, and we had carefully
shot their wreckers and plunderers. But no modern traveller had ven-
tured into the wild depths, and we were driven for information to the
pages of old Father Lobo, of Mr. Salt, and of M. de Rienzi.[5]

And my project aimed at something higher. I had read in Ptolemy
(I.9) the following words: "Then concerning the navigation between the
Aromata Promontory [i.e., Guardafui] and Rhapta [the 'place of seven
ships,' generally supposed to be north of Kilwa], Marinus of Tyre
declares that a certain Diogenes, one of those sailing to India . . . when
near Aromata and having the Troglodytic region on the right [some of
the Somall were still cave-dwellers], reached, after twenty-five days'

---

5 Translations of Father Jerome Lobo's accounts were published under the titles
   A short relation of the River Nile, of its source and currents (1669) and *A Voyage to
   Abyssinia* (1735). Other references are to Henry Salt, *A Voyage to Abyssinia . . .
   in the years 1809 and 1810* (1814) and Domeny De Rienzi, *Dictionaire usuel et
   scientifique de géographie* (Paris, 1840).

march, the lakes [plural and not dual] whence the Nile flows and of which Point Rhapta is a little south."[6]

This remarkable passage was to me a revelation; it was the *mot de l'enigme,* the way to make the egg stand upright, the rending of the veil of Isis. The feat for which Julius Caesar would have relinquished a civil war, the secret which kings from Nero to Mahommed Ali vainly attempted to solve, the discovery for which travellers, from Herodotus to Bruce,[7] have risked their lives, was reduced to comparative facility. For the last 300 years explorers had been working, literally and metaphorically, against the stream, where disease and savagery had exhausted health and energy, pocket and patience, at the very beginning of the end. I therefore resolved to reverse the operation, and thus I hoped to see the young Nile and to stultify a certain old proverb.[8]

The then Court of Directors [of the East India Company] unwillingly sanctioned my project: I was too clever by half, and they suspected that it concealed projects of annexation or conquest. All that my political views aimed at was to secure the supremacy of my country in the Red Sea. Despite Lord Palmerston and Robert Stephenson, I foresaw that the Suez Canal would be a success;[9] and I proposed to purchase for the sum of

---

6   Burton's library contained: Claudii Ptolemaei, *Geographia,* ed. C. F. A. Nobbe (Leipzig,1843). The translation here is presumably by Burton. "English," he remarked, "is almost the only European tongue which has not translated the immortal 'Geographia'" (*Camoens: His Life and His Lusiads. A Commentary* [London, 1881], 1:275n). He also maintained that his own explorations in Africa vindicated Ptolemy's account. Burton's commentary within the quotation is enclosed here within squared brackets.

7   James Bruce recorded his experience in *Travels to Discover the Source of the Nile in the years 1768 . . . to 1773* (1790). In *First Footsteps in East Africa* (1856), Burton remarked: "It is now the fashion to laud Bruce, and to pity his misfortunes. I cannot but think that he deserved them" (ed. Gordon Waterfield [New York, 1966], 181n; subsqent page references are to this edition). Burton provided a more balanced account in "Notes on the Dahoman" (1865), remarking that "the great Abyssinian traveller took his place as a man with a solid foundation of merit, and with less than the average amount of error" (*Selected Papers on Anthropology, Travel & Exploration,* ed. N. M. Penzer [London, 1924], 125).

8   "Facilius sit Nili caput invenire" (It would be easier to discover the source of the Nile).

9   Robert Stephenson (1803-1859) was the English representative in the Société d'Études du Canal de Suez in 1846. He argued that a railroad would be more practical than a canal, and in 1851 he headed a group to establish the railroad. As a member of Parliament after 1847, Stephenson supported Palmerston's opposition to the canal.

£10,000 all the ports on the East African shore, as far south as Berbera. This was refused, I was sternly reprimanded and—the result will presently appear.[10]

In July of the same year we reached Aden. Our little party was composed of Lieutenant Herne and Lieutenant Stroyan, with myself in command. Before setting out I permitted Lieutenant J. H. Speke to join us; he was in search of African sport, and, being a stranger, he was glad to find companions. This officer afterwards accompanied me to Central Africa, and died at Bath on Thursday, September 15th, 1864.

Aden, the "Eye of Yemen," or the "Coal Hole of the East" (as we call it), the "dry and squalid city" of Abulfeda, gave me much trouble. It is one of the worst, if not the worst, places of residence to which Anglo-Indian employés are condemned. The town occupies the crater floor of an extinct volcano whose northern wall, a grim block of bare black basalt known as Jebel Shamsham, is said to be the sepulchre of Kabil, or Cain, and certainly the First Murderer lies in an appropriate spot. Between May and October the climate is dreadful, the storms of unclean dust necessitate candles at noon, and not a drop of rain falls, whilst high in the red hot air you see the clouds rolling towards the highlands of the interior, where their blessed loads will make Arabia happy. In Yemen —Arabia Felix—there are bubbling springs and fruits and vineyards, sweet waters, fertilising suns, and cool nights. In Aden and its neighbourhood all is the abomination of desolation.

The miseries of our unfortunate troops might have been lightened had we originally occupied the true key of the Red Sea, the port of Berbera on the Somali coast opposite Aden. But the step had been taken; the authorities would not cry "Peccavi"[11] and undo the past. Therefore

---

10 In an "Official Report" (22 February 1855), Burton recommended that a commercial agency be established at Berbera, and he reiterated this in a letter to the secretary of the Royal Geographical Society (15 December 1856) which was forwarded to government officials. In response, the secretary to the government at Bombay wrote (23 July 1857): "Your want of discretion, and due respect for the authorities to whom you are subordinate, has been regarded with displeasure" (Burton, *The Lake Regions of Central Africa* [London, 1860], 2: 422-28). In his lecture, Burton indicates that the failure to protect British interests resulted in the final attack on his expedition. In 1884, he probably felt vindicated when the British occupied Berbera. In his copy of *First Footsteps in East Africa* (Burton Library no. 7, in the Huntington Library), he has pasted in a newspaper clipping from *The Graphic* (26 July 1884) concerned with this event. The article concludes: "Perhaps the best account of the race will be found in Burton's 'First Footsteps in East Africa.' "

11 "I have sinned"—a tag associated with Sir Charles Napier (1782-1853) after his controversial conquest of Sind in 1843.

we died of fever and dysentery; the smallest wound became a fearful ulcer which destroyed limb or life. Even in health, existence without appetite or sleep was a pest. I had the audacity to publish these facts, and had once more to pay the usual penalty for telling the truth.[12]

The English spirit suffers from confinement behind any but wooden walls, and the Aden garrison displayed a timidity which astonished me. The fierce faces, the screaming voices, and the frequent faction-fights of the savage Somal had cowed our countrymen, and they were depressed by a "peace-at-any-price" policy. Even the Brigadier Commanding, General (afterwards Sir) James Outram, opposed the exploration, and the leader was represented to be a madman leading others to a certain and cruel death.

I at once changed my plans: to prove that the journey presented no real danger, I offered to visit alone what was considered the most perilous part of the country and to explore Harar, the Capital of a *Terra Incognita*. But to prevent my being detained in the interim I stationed my companions on the African coast with orders to seize and stop the inland Caravans—a measure which would have had the effect of releasing me. This is a serious danger in Abyssinian travel: witness the cases of Pedro Covilhao in 1499, and the unfortunate Consul Cameron in our own day.[13] Those "nameless Ethiopians," the older savages, sacrificed strangers to their gods. The modern only keep them in irons, flog them, and starve them.

In that day few but professed geographers knew even the name of Harar, or suspected that within 300 miles of Aden there was a counterpart of ill-famed Timbuktu. Travellers of all nations had attempted it in vain—men of science, missionaries, and geographers had all failed. It was said that some Hamitic prophet had read Decline and Fall in the First Footsteps of the Frank, and that the bigoted barbarians had threatened death to the Infidel caught within their walls. Yet it was worth seeing, especially in these days, when few are the unvisited cities of the world. It has a stirring history, a peculiar race and language, it coins its

---

12 *First Footsteps in East Africa*, 229-30.
13 In *First Footsteps in East Africa*, Burton wrote: "The Abyssinian law of detaining guests—Pedro Covilhaõ, the first Portuguese envoy (A.D. 1499), lived and died a prisoner there—appears to have been the Christian modification of the old Ethiopic rite of sacrificing strangers" (46n). According to Charles T. Beke, Captain Cameron, the British Consul at Massowah, had been held captive in Abyssinia for more than a year (*The British Captives in Abyssinia* [London, 1865], 1).

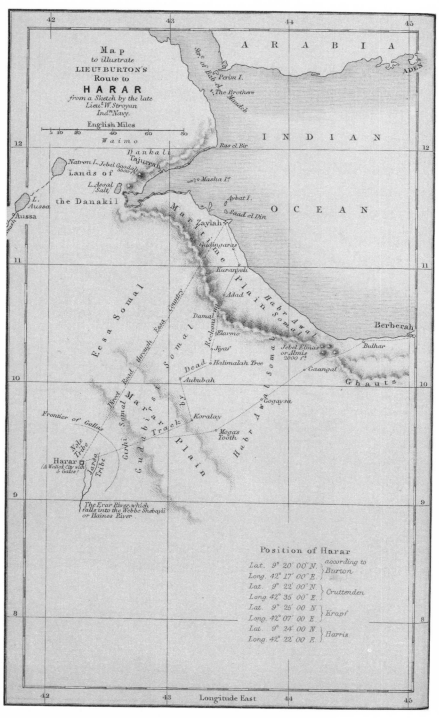

Route to Harar. From *First Footsteps in East Africa* (1856).

own money, and it exports the finest coffee known. Finally it is the south-ernmost native town in Tropical Africa: beyond it, to the Cape of Good Hope all the settlements are huts and hide-tents, and most of them are temporary.

On April 28th, 1854, in an open boat, I left Aden, re-becoming El Hajj Abdullah, the Arab. My attendants were Mohammed and Gulad, two Somali policemen bound to keep my secret for the safety of their own throats. I afterwards engaged one Abdy Abokr, a kind of hedge-priest, whose nickname was the "End of Time," meaning the *ne plus ultra* of villainy. He was a caution—a bad tongue, a mischievous brain, covetous and wasteful, treacherous as a hyena, revengeful as a camel, timorous as a jackal.

Three days of summer sail over the "blind billows" and the "singing waves" of the romantic Arab geographers landed us at Zayla, alias Audal, the classical Sinus Avaliticus, to the south-west of Aden. During the seventh century it was the capital of a kingdom which measured forty-three by forty days' march; now the Bedouin ride up to its walls. The site is the normal Arabo-African scene, a strip of sulphur-yellow sand with a deep blue dome above and a foreground of indigo-coloured sea; behind it lies the country, a reeking desert of loose white sand and brown clay, thinly scattered with thorny shrub and tree. The buildings are a dozen large houses of mud and coralline-rubble painfully white-washed; there are six mosques, green little battlemented things with the Wahhali dwarf tower by way of minaret, and two hundred huts of dingy palm-leaf.

The population of 1,500 souls has not a good name—"Zayla boasting (or vanity) and Kurayesh pride" is a proverb. They are managed by forty Turkish soldiers under a Somali Governor, the Hajj Sharmarkay, meaning "one who sees no harm." The tall old man was a brave in his youth; he could manage four spears, and his sword-cut was known. He always befriended English travellers.

The only thing in favour of Zayla is its cheapness: a family of six persons lives well on £30 per annum. Being poor, the people are idle, and the hateful "Inshalla bukra"—"To-morrow if Allah pleases"—[and] the Arab "tenha paciencia," "amanho," and "espere um pouco" is the rule.

I was delayed twenty-seven days whilst a route was debated upon, mules were sent for, camels were bought, and an "Abban," or Protector-guide, was secured. Hereabouts no stranger can travel without such

Mohammed Mahmud, also known as the "Hammal," or porter. From *First Footsteps in East Africa* (1856).

patron, who is paid to defend his client's life and property. Practically he takes his money and he runs away.

On the morning of November 27th, 1854, the Caravan was ready. It consisted of five camels laden with provisions, cooking-pots, ammunition, and our money—that is to say, beads, coarse tobacco, American sheeting, Indian cotton, and indigo-dyed stuffs. The escort is formed by the two policemen, the "End of Time," and Yusuf, a one-eyed lad from Zayla, with the guide and his tail of three followers. My men are the pink of Somali fashion. They have stained their hair of a light straw colour by plastering it with ashes; they have teased it till it stands up a full foot, and they have mutually spirted upon their wigs melted tallow, making their heads look like giant cauliflowers that contrast curiously with the bistre-coloured skins. Their tobes (togas) are dazzlingly white, with borders dazzlingly red. Outside the dress is strapped a horn-hilted two-edged dagger, long and heavy; their shields of rhinoceros hide are bran-new, and their two spears poised upon the right shoulder are freshly scraped and oiled, and blackened and polished. They have added my spare rifle and guns to the camel loads—the things are well enough at Aden, but in Somaliland men would deride such strange, unmanly weapons. They balance themselves upon dwarf Abyssinian saddles, extending the leg and raising the heel like the *haute école* of Louis XIV. The stirrup is an iron ring admitting only the big toe, and worse than that of the Sertanejo.

As usual in this country, where the gender masculine will not work, we have two cooks—tall, buxom, muscular dames, chocolate skinned and round faced. They had curiously soft and fluted voices, hardly to be expected from their square and huge-hipped figures, and contrasting agreeably with the harsh organs of the men. Their feet are bare, their waist is confined by a narrow fillet, and the body-cloth is an indigo-dyed cotton, girt at the waist and graceful as a winding sheet. I never saw them eat; probably, as the people say of cooks, they lived by sucking their fingers.

And here a few words about the Somal, amongst whom we are to travel. These nomads are not pure negroes; like the old Egyptians, they are a mixed breed of African and Arab. The face, from the brow to the nostrils, is Asiatic; from the nostrils to the chin there are traces of negro blood. The hair is African; they imitate it by a sheepskin wig cut to the head and died fiery orange with henna—it certainly does no honour to the patronage of Saint Louis (1267).[14] The figure is peculiar, the shoulders are high and narrow, the trunk is small, the limbs are spider-like, and the forearm is often of simian proportions.

The Somali are a free people, lawless as free. The British Government will not sanction their being sold as slaves. Of course they enslave others, and they have a servile caste called "Midyan," who are the only archers. They have little reverence for their own chiefs except in council, and they discuss every question in public, none hesitating to offer the wildest conjectures. At different times, they suggested that I was a Turk, an Egyptian, a Meccah man, a Banyan,[15] Ahmad the Indian, the Governor of Aden, a merchant, a pilgrim, the chief of Zayla or his son, a boy, a warrior in silver armour, an old woman, a man painted white, and lastly, a calamity sent down from heaven to tire out the lives of the Somal.

The Somal are bad Moslems, but they believe in a Deity and they know the name of their Prophet. Wives being purchased for their value in cows or camels, the wealthy old are polygamous and the young poor are, perforce, bachelors. They work milk-pots of tree-fibre like the beer-basket of Kaffirland distant 1500 miles. They are not bad smiths, but they confine their work to knives, spear-heads, and neat bits for their unshod horses. As the Kaffirs, they call bright iron "rotten," and they never temper it. Like all Africans, they are very cruel riders.

These nomads have a passion for independence, and yet when placed under a strong arm they are easily disciplined. In British Aden a merry, laughing, dancing, and fighting race, at home they are a moping and melancholy people—for this their lives of perpetual danger may account. This insecurity makes them truly hard-hearted. I have seen them when shifting camp barbarously leave behind for the hyenas their sick and decrepit parents. When the fatal smallpox breaks out, the first cases are often speared and the huts burned over the still warm corpses.

The Somal deem nothing so noble as murder. The more cowardly the deed is, the better, as showing the more "nous." Even the midnight butchery of a sleeping guest is highly honourable. The hero plants a "rish," or white ostrich feather, in his tufty pole and walks about the admired of all admirers, whilst the wives of those who have not received

---

14 Saint Louis (canonized 1297) had attacked Moslem headquarters in Egypt in 1247 and ascended the Nile as far as Massourah before retreating.

15 In *The Lake Regions of Central Africa,* Burton described the Banyan as "a race national as the English, who do their best to import into Eastern Africa the cows and curries, the customs and the costumes, of Western India" (1:19).

this order of merit taunt their husbands as *noirs fainéants* [black idlers]. Curious to say, the Greek and Roman officers used to present these plumes to the bravest soldiers for wearing on the helmet.

My journey began with the hard alluvial plain, forty-five to fifty-eight miles broad, between the sea and the mountains. It belongs to the Eesa, a tribe of Somali Bedouin, and how these "sun-dwellers" can exist there is a mystery. On the second day we reached a kraal consisting of "Gurgi," or diminutive hide huts. There was no thorn fence as is required in the lion-haunted lands to the west. The scene was characteristic of that pastoral life which supplies poetry with Arcadian images and history with its blackest tragedies. Whistling shepherds, tall thin men, spear in hand, bore the younglings of the herd in their bosoms or drove to pasture the long-necked camels preceded by a patriarch with a wooden bell. Patches of Persian sheep with snowy bodies and jetty faces flecked the tawny plain, and flocks of goats were committed to women dressed in skins and boys who are unclad till the days of puberty. Some led the ram, around whose neck a cord of white heather was tied for luck. Others frisked with the dogs, animals by no means contemptible in the eyes of these Bedouin Moslems. All begged for "Bori"—the precious tobacco—their only narcotic. They run away if they see you smoke, and they suspect a kettle to be a mortal weapon—so the Bachwanas (Bichuanas) call our cannon, "pots." Many of these wild people have never tasted grain and have never heard of coffee or sugar. During the rains they live on milk; in the dries they eat meat, avoiding, however, the blood. Like other races to the north and south, they will not touch fish or birds, which they compare with snakes and vultures. "Speak not to me with that mouth which has tasted fish!" is a dire insult.

The Eesa [are] a typical Somali tribe; it may number 100,000 spears, and it has a bad name. "Treacherous as an Eesa," is a proverb at Zayla, where it is said that these savages will offer you a bowl of milk with the left hand and will stab you with the right. Their lives are spent in battle and murder.

The next march, a total of fifty-two miles, nearly lost us. Just before reaching the mountains which subtend the coast, we crossed the warm trail of a Razzia, or Cavalcade: some 200 of the Habr Awal, our inveterate enemies, had been scouring the country. Robinson Crusoe was less scared by the footprint than were my companions. Our weak party numbered only nine men, of whom all except Mohammed and Gulad were useless, and the first charge would have been certain death.

Escaping this danger, we painfully endured the rocks and thorns of the mountains and wilds. The third march placed us at Halimalah, a sacred tree about half-way between this coast and our destination —Harar. It is a huge sycamore suggesting the "hiero-sykaminon" of Egypt. The Gallas are still tree-worshippers, and the Somal respect this venerable vegetable as do the English their Druidical mistletoe.[16]

We are well received at the "Ker" (the kraals or villages). They are fenced with large and terrible thorns, an effectual defence against bare-legged men. The animals have a place apart; the proprietors occupy small semi-circular beehives made of grass mats mounted on sticks. The furniture consists of weapons, hides, wooden pillows and mats for beds, pots of woven fibre, and horse gear. We carry our own dates and rice, we buy meat and the people supply us with milk gratis—to sell it is a disgrace. Fresh milk is drunk only by the civilised; pastoral people prefer it when artificially curdled and soured, the "Coalhado" of Brazil.

We soon rise high above sea-level, as the cold nights and the burning suns told us. The eighth march placed us on the "Barr Marar," a plain twenty-seven miles broad—at that season a waterless stubble, a yellow nap, dotted with thorny trees and bushes, and at all times infamous for robbery and murder. It is a glorious place for game: in places it is absolutely covered with antelopes, and every random shot must tell in the immense herds.

Here I had the displeasure of being stalked by a lion. As night drew in we were urging our jaded mules over the western prairie towards a dusky line of hills. My men preceded whilst I rode in rear with a double-barrelled gun at full cock across my knees. Suddenly my animal trembled and bolted forward with a sidelong glance of fear. I looked back and saw, within some twenty yards, the King of Beasts creeping up, silently as a cat. To fire both barrels in the direction of my stalker was the work of a second. I had no intention of hitting, as aim could not be taken in the gloaming, and to wound would have been fatal. The flame and the echoed roar from the hills made my friend slink away. Its intention was, doubtless, to crawl within springing distance and then by a bound on my neck to have finished my journey through Somaliland and through

---

16 Burton considered the Somal to be "a half-caste tribe, an offshoot of the great Galla race" (*First Footsteps in East Africa*, 88). By his account, the Gallas were named after the river Gala, where they had vanquished their kinsmen, the Abyssinians.

life. My companions shouted in horror "Libah! Libah!"—"The lion! the lion!"—and saw a multitude of lions that night.

After crossing the desert prairie, we entered the hills of the agricultural Somal, the threshold of the South Abyssinian mountains. The pastoral scene now changed for waving crops of millet, birds in flights, and hedged lanes, where I saw with pleasure the dog-rose. Guided by a wild fellow called "Abtidon," we passed on to Sagharrah, the village of the Gerad, or Chief, "Adan." He has not a good name, and I was afterwards told he was my principal danger. But we never went anywhere without our weapons, and the shooting of a few vultures on the wing was considered a great feat where small shot is unknown. "He brings down birds from the sky!" exclaimed the people.

I must speak of the Gerad, however, as I found him—a civil and hospitable man, greedy of course, suspicious, and of shortsighted policy. His good and pretty wife Khayrah was very kind, and supplied me with abundance of honey-wine, the "merissa" of Abyssinia. It tasted like champagne to a palate long condemned to total abstinence, without even tea.

We were now within thirty direct miles of Harar, and my escort made a dead stand. "Adan" naturally wanted to monopolise us and our goods. My men, therefore, were threatened with smallpox, the bastinado, life-long captivity in unlit dungeons, and similar amenities.

On January 2nd, 1855, I sent for our mules. They were missing. An unpleasantness was the consequence, and the animals appeared about noon. I saddled my own—no one would assist me. When, mounted and gun in hand, I rode up to my followers, who sat sulkily on the ground, and observing that hitherto their acts had not been those of the brave, I suggested that before returning to Aden we should do something of manliness. They arose, begged me not to speak such words, and offered to advance if I would promise to reward them should we live and to pay blood-money to their friends in case of the other contingency. They apparently attached much importance to what is vulgarly termed "cutting up well."

Now, however, we were talking reason, and I settled all difficulties by leaving a letter addressed to the Political Resident at Aden. Mohammed and Gulad were chosen to accompany me, the rest remaining with the Gerad "Adan." I must say for my companions that once in the saddle they shook off all their fears; they were fatalists, and they

Harar from the Goffe Stream. From *First Footsteps in East Africa* (1856).

believed in my star, whilst they had the fullest confidence in their pay or pension.

The country now became romantic and beautiful—a confusion of lofty stony mountains, plantations of the finest coffee, scatters of villages, forests of noble trees, with rivulets of the coolest and clearest water. We here stood some 5,500 feet high, and although only 9° degrees removed from the Line, the air was light and pleasant as that of San Paulo. It made me remember the climate of Aden, and hate it.

We slept en route, and on January 3rd we first sighted Harar City. On the crest of a hill distant two miles it appeared, a long sombre line strikingly contrasting with the whitewashed settlements of the more civilised East, and nothing broke the outline except the two grey and rudely shaped minarets of the Jami, or Matriz (cathedral). I almost grudged the exposure of three lives to win so paltry a prize. But of all that have attempted but one has succeeded in entering that ugly pile of stone.

We then approached the city gate and sat there, as is the custom, till invited to enter. Presently we were ordered to the Palace by a chamberlain, a man with loud and angry voice and eyes. At the entrance we dismounted by command, and we were told to run across the court—which I refused to do. We were then placed under a tree in one corner of the yard and to the right of the Palace: the latter is a huge, windowless barn of rough stone and red clay without other insignia but a thin coat of whitewash over the doorway.

Presently we were beckoned in and told to doff our slippers. A curtain was raised, and we stood in the presence of the then Amir of Harar, Sultan Ahmad bin Sultan Abibakr.

The sight was savage, if not imposing. The hall of audience was a dark room, eighty to ninety feet long, and its whitewashed walls were hung with rusty fetters and bright matchlocks. At the further end, on a common East Indian cane sofa, sat a small yellow personage—the great man. He wore a flowing robe of crimson cloth edged with snowy fur, and a narrow white turban twisted round a tall conical cap of red velvet. Ranged in double ranks perpendicular to the presence and nearest to the chief were his favourites and courtiers, with right arms bared after the fashion of Abyssinia. Prolonging these parallel lines towards the door were Galla warriors, wild men with bushy wigs. Shining rings of zinc on their arms, wrists, and ankles formed their principal attire. They stood motionless as statues, not an eye moved, and each right hand held upright a spear with an enormous head of metal, the heel being planted in the ground.

I entered with a loud "As 'Salamu alaykum"—"Peace be upon ye!" —and the normal answer was returned. A pair of chamberlains then led me forward to bow over the chief's hand. He directed me to sit upon a mat opposite him, and with lowering brow and inquisitive glance he asked what might be my business at Harar. It was the crisis. I introduced myself as an Englishman from Aden coming to report that certain changes had taken place there, in the hope that the "cordial intent" might endure between the Kingdoms of Harar and England.

The Amir smiled graciously. I must own that the smile was a relief to me. It was a joy to my attendants, who sat on the ground behind their master, grey-brown with emotion, and mentally inquiring, "What next?"

The audience over, we were sent to one of the Amir's houses, distant about one hundred paces from the Palace. Here cakes of soured maize (fuba), soaked in curdled milk, and lumps of beef plentifully powdered with pepper, awaited us. Then we were directed to call upon Gerad Mohammed, Premier of Harar. He received us well, and we retired to rest not dissatisfied with that afternoon's work. We had eaten the chief's bread and salt.

During my ten days' stay at Harar I carefully observed the place and its people. The city is walled and pierced with five large gates, flanked by towers, but ignorant of cannon. The streets—narrow lanes strewed with rocks and rubbish—are formed by houses built of granite and sandstone from the adjacent mountains. The best abodes are double storied, long and flat roofed, with holes for windows placed jealously high up, and the doors are composed of a single plank. The women, I need hardly say, have separate apartments. The city abounds in mosques—plain buildings without minarets—and the graveyards are stuffed with tombs, oblongs formed by slabs planted edgeways in the ground.

The people, numbering about 8,000 souls, have a bad name amongst their neighbours. The Somal say that Harar is a "Paradise inhabited by asses"; and "hard as the heart of Harar" is a byword. The junior members of the royal family are imprisoned till wanted for the throne. Amongst the men I did not see a single handsome face or hear one pleasant voice. The features are harsh and plain, the skin is a sickly yellowish brown, the hair and beard are short and intractable, and the hands and feet are large and coarse. They are celebrated for laxity of morals, fondness for strong waters, much praying, coffee-drinking, and chewing tobacco and "Kat," a well-known theine plant.[17] They have a considerable commerce with the coast, which is reached by a large caravan once a year.

The women are beautiful by the side of their lords. They have small heads, regular profiles, straight noses, large eyes, mouths almost Caucasian, and light brown skins. The hair, parted in the centre and gathered into two large bunches behind the ears, is covered with dark blue muslin or network, whose ends were tied under the chin. Girls collect their locks, which are long, thick, and wavy—not wiry—into a knot à la Diane; a curtain of short close plaits escaping from the bunch falls upon the shoulders. The dress is a wide frock of chocolate or indigo-dyed cotton, girt round the middle with a sash; before and behind there is a triangle of scarlet with the point downwards. The ornaments are earrings and necklaces of silver for the rich: the poor content themselves with red beads. On the forearm are six or seven circles of black buffalo horn, the work of Western India. The bosom is tattooed with stars, the eyebrows are lengthened with dyes, the eyes are fringed with antimony,

---

17 In *First Footsteps in East Africa,* Burton quoted from *Pharmaceutical Journal* a description of Kât as "a pleasurable excitant." "When chewed . . . ," continues the account, "[it is] said to produce great hilarity of spirits and an agreeable state of wakefulness" (p. 299).

and the palms and soles are stained red. Those pretty faces have harsh voices, their manners are rude, and I regret to say that an indiscreet affection for tobacco and honey wine sometimes leads to a public bastinado.

[At] Harar is a university which supplies Somaliland with poor scholars and crazy priests. There are no endowments for students—learning is its own reward—and books (manuscripts) are rare and costly. Only theology is studied. Some of the graduates have made a name in the Holy Land of Arabia, where few rank higher than my friend Shaykh Jami el Berteri. To be on the safer side he would never touch tobacco or coffee. I liked his conversation, but I eschewed his dinners.

Harar—called "Gay" or "Harar Gay" by her sons—is the capital of Hadiyah, a province of the ancient Zayla empire, and her fierce Moslems nearly extirpated Christianity from Shoa and Amhara. The local Attila, Mohammed Gragne, or the "Left-Handed," slew in 1540 David III, the last Ethiopian monarch who styled himself "King of Kings."

David's successor, Claudius, sent imploring messages to Europe, and D. Joaõ III. ordered the chivalrous Stephen and Christopher da Gama, sons of Vasco da Gama, to the rescue. The Portuguese could oppose only 350 muskets and a rabble rout of Abyssinians to 10,000 Moslems. D. Christopher was wounded, taken prisoner, and decapitated. Good Father Lobo declares that "where the martyr's head fell, a fountain sprung up of wonderful virtue, which cured many hopeless diseases."

Eventually Gragne was shot by one Pedro Leaõ, a Portuguese soldier who was bent upon revenging his leader's fall. The Moslem's wife, Talwambara, prevented the dispersion of the army by making a slave personate her dead husband, and drew off her forces in safety. A strong-minded woman!

My days at Harar were dull enough. At first we were visited by all the few strangers in the city, but they soon thought it prudent to shun us. The report of my "English brethren" being on the coast made them look upon me as a "mufsid," or dangerous man. The Somal, on the other hand, in compliment to my attendants, were most attentive. It was harvest home, and we had an opportunity of seeing the revels of the threshers and reapers—a jovial race, slightly "dipsomaniac."

Harar also is the great half-way house and resting place for slaves between Abyssinia and the coast. In making purchases, the adage is, "If you want a brother in battle, buy a Nubian; if you would be rich, an Abyssinian; if you require an ass, a negro."

I sometimes called upon the learned and religious, but not willingly
—these Shaykhash, or Reverend men, had proposed detaining me until
duly converted and favoured with a "call." Harar, like most African
cities, was a prison on a large scale. "You enter by your own will; you
leave by another's," is the pithy saw.

At length, when really anxious to depart, and when my two Somal
had consulted their rosaries for the thousandth time, I called upon the
Gerad Mohammed, who had always been civil to me. He was suffering
from a chronic bronchitis. Here, then, lay my chance of escaping from my
rat-trap. The smoke of some brown paper matches steeped in saltpetre
relieved him. We at once made a bargain. The minister was to take me
before his chief and secure for me a ceremonious dismissal. On the other
part, I bound myself to send up from the coast a lifelong supply of the
precious medicine. We both kept faith. Moreover, after returning to Aden
I persuaded the authorities to reward with handsome presents the men
who held my life in their hands, and yet who did not take it.

After a pleasing interview with the Amir, who did his best to smile,
we left Harar on January 13th, 1855. At Sagharrah, where the villagers
had prayed the death-prayer as we set out for the city, we were received
with effusion. They now scattered over us handfuls of roasted grain, and
they danced with delight, absorbing copious draughts of liquor. The
"End of Time" nearly wept crocodile's tears, and the women were grateful that their charms had not been exposed to the terrible smallpox.

After a week's rest we prepared to make the coast. I was desirous of
striking Berbera, a port south of Zayla, where my friends awaited me.
The escort consented to accompany me by the short direct road, on condition of travelling night and day. They warned me that they had a blood
feud with all the tribes on the path, that we should find very little water
and no provisions, and that the heat would be frightful. Truly, a pleasant
prospect for a weary man!

But if *they* could stand it, so could I. The weaker attendants, the
women, and the camels were sent back by the old path, and I found
myself en route on January 26th, accompanied by my three Somal and by
a wild guide known as Dubayr—the "Donkey." My provaunt [proviant]
for five days consisted of five biscuits, a few limes, and sundry lumps of
sugar.

I will not deny that that ride was trying work. The sun was fearful,
the nights were raw and damp. For twenty-four hours we did not taste

water; our brains felt baked, our throats burned, the mirage mocked us at every turn, and the effect was a kind of monomania. At length a small bird showed us a well and prevented, I believe, our going mad. The scenery was uniform and uninteresting—horrid hills upon which withered aloes raised their spears; plains apparently rained upon by showers of fire and stones, and rolling ground rich only in "wait a bit" thorns, made to rend man's skin and garment. We scrupulously avoided the Kraals, and when on one occasion the wild people barred the way we were so intolerably fierce with hunger and thirst that they fled from us as if we were fiends. The immortal Ten Thousand certainly did not sight the cold waters of the Euxine with more delight than we felt when hailing the warm bay of Berbera.[18] I ended that toilsome ride to and from Harar of 240 miles at 2 a.m. on January 30th, 1855, after a last spell of 40 miles equal to 80 in Brazil. A glad welcome from my brother expeditionists soon made amends for past privations and fatigues.

And now to recount the most unpleasant part of my first adventure in East Africa.

Having paid a visit to Aden, I returned to Berbera in April, 1855, prepared to march upon the head waters of the Nile.

But Fate and the British authorities were against me. I had done too much—I had dared to make Berbera a rival port. They were not scrupulous at Aden, even to the taking of life.

My little party consisted of forty-two muskets, including three officers and myself. The men, however, were not to be trusted, but after repeated applications I could not obtain an escort of Somali policemen. Matters looked ugly, and the more so as there was no retreat.

The fair of Berbera, which had opened in early October, was breaking up, and the wild clansmen were retiring from the seaboard to their native hills. The harbour rapidly emptied; happily, however, for us, a single boat remained there.

We slept comfortably on April 18th, agreeing to have a final shot at the gazelles before marching. Between 2 a.m. and 3 a.m. we were aroused by a rush of men like the roar of a stormy wind. I learned afterwards that our enemies numbered between three and four hundred. We armed ourselves with all speed, whilst our party, after firing a single volley, ran away as quickly as possible.

---

18   A reference to the elite of the Persian army whose numbers were kept constant by replacement of those injured or killed in battle.

The unfortunate Lieutenant Stroyan was run through with a spear; he slept far from us, and we did not see him fall. Lieutenants Herne and Speke and I defended ourselves in our tent till the savages proceeded to beat it down. I then gave the word to sally out and cleared the way with my sabre. Lieutenant Herne accompanied me and—wonderful to relate! —escaped without injury. Lieutenant Speke was seized and tied up; he had eleven spear-thrusts before he could free himself, and he escaped by a miracle. When outside the camp, I vainly tried once more to bring up our men to the fray. Finding me badly hurt they carried me on board the boat. Here I was presently joined by the survivors, who carried with them the corpse of our ill-fated friend.

Sad and dispirited, we returned to Aden. We had lost our property as well as our blood, and I knew too well that we should be rewarded with nothing but blame. The authorities held a Court of Inquiry in my absence, and facetiously found that we and not they were in fault. Lord Dalhousie, the admirable statesman then Governing in General British India, declared that they were quite right. I begin to think that they were.

Such, ladies and gentlemen, is the plain unvarnished account of what "led to the Discovery of the Nile-Sources."

Lecture 4
A Mission to Dahome

Introduction

In 1861, Burton was appointed consul at Fernando Po, an island off the coast of West Africa where Britain maintained a base which aimed to suppress the slave trade. Burton had hoped for the consulship at Damascus—a post granted to him in 1868—and he was not at first pleased by the prospect of Fernando Po. He declared that the climate was pestilential—the region, a suitable place to take a wife only if a man wanted to rid himself of her. (Burton, who had been married seven months, prudently left his wife in England.) However, the region was the starting point for some challenging explorations. Soon after arriving there, he set off for Abeokuta, the capital of Nigeria, and he followed this excursion with some climbing in the Cameroon Mountains and some unsuccessful gorilla hunting along the Gabon River. Like most of Burton's journeys, these experiences led to several two-volume narratives: *Wandering in West Africa from Liverpool to Fernando Po* (1863), *Abeokuta and the Camaroons Mountains* (1863), and *Two Trips to Gorilla Land and the Cataracts of the Congo* (1876). In addition, Burton made two journeys to Dahomey. The first visit (18 May-17 June 1863) was unofficial and unknown even to the Foreign Office; the second (2 December 1863 to 26 February 1864) was an official mission intended to turn King Gelele from the practices of human sacrifice and slave trading. These experiences also led to a two-volume publication: *A Mission to Gelele, King of Dahome* (1864).

Burton may have chosen to lecture on Dahomey because his Brazilian audience had close connections with the area as a result of the slave trade. In *Dahomey and the Dahomans* (1851), Frederick E. Forbes wrote of "the annual introduction of 60,000 slaves in Brazil" (p. 138). Beside this passage, Burton has written in the margin of his copy: "None"—referring to the changed situation of the mid-1860s. There remained, however, an estimated 1,400,000 to 1,700,000 slaves in Brazil, according to a commentator on the topic during Burton's years in South America.[1] This might well seem to have posed for Burton a delicate situation. However, among his varying remarks on slavery, he emphasized the importance of

---

1 A. M. Perdiago Malheiro, "The Extinction of Slavery in Brazil from a practical point of view," Anthropological Review 6.20 (January 1868): 56-63.

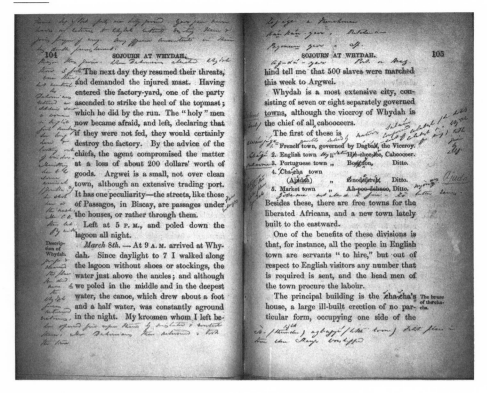

Annotations to F. E. Forbes's *Dahomey and the Dahomans* (1851), Burton Library no. 1574.

an "historical" understanding. Slavery, he declared, to be "almost universally a concomitant of a certain state of civilization."[2] This interpretation —and a corresponding turn from a central moral concern—must have been quite acceptable to Burton's original listeners.

The British were also quite familiar with Dahomey. Its connection with the slave trade and its "savage" practices had attracted considerable attention, and a good deal had been written about it. As Burton's library indicates, he knew the primary publications well. It contains Archibald Dalzel's *The History of Dahomy* (1793), John M'Leod's *A Voyage to Africa, with some account of the manners and customs of the Dahomian People* (1820), John Duncan's *Travels in Western Africa, in 1845 and 1846* (1847), and Frederick E. Forbes's *Dahomey and the Dahomans* (1851). All of these volumes contain Burton's marginalia. At some points, his comments are sharp. "Three contradictions in 3 pages," he notes in Forbes's *Dahomey and the Dahomans*. "Something to boast of." Or, more curtly: "Rot." At

2　Richard Burton, *A Mission to Gelele, King of Dahome* (London, 1864), 2:19.

other points, he indicates approval by a schoolmasterly: "Good."

Burton was especially critical of those writers who had both romanti-cized and sensationalized their accounts of Dahomey. Where other writ-ers had found in court practices a "barbaric splendour," he found only "barren barbarism."[3] The number of human sacrifices during the notori-ous "customs," though "terribly great," had, according to Burton, been "much swollen by report."[4] Similarly, he remarked on the "chronic exag-geration touching the mis-called 'Amazons' [which] has of late years pre-vailed in England";[5] this female army was neither so numerous nor so formidable as commonly reported. In such analysis, Burton was clearly intent on presenting himself as a responsible ethnographer. He had, after all, declared in *The Lake Regions of Central Africa* (London, 1860) that the ethnology of Africa was "its most interesting, if not its only interesting feature" (1:107).

Burton was obviously not so dispassionate or unprejudiced a com-mentator as he would have us believe. His assumption of racial superior-ity, which he shared with virtually all of his contemporaries with similar background, is apparent in the lecture, for example, in his reference to Africans as "savages and barbarians" and, even more pronouncedly, in his reference to "the anthropoid" of West Africa. Burton also displays animus in his remarks on "amiable philanthropists"—and it seems likely that some of his derogatory remarks on Africans, reprehensible in any case by our standards, were deliberately intended to annoy these indi-viduals. In particular, he ridiculed the philanthropists' notion of slavery as "the sum of all villainies." But the frequency of such attacks alone makes them seem suspect. (He even dedicated *Wanderings in Africa* [1863] "To the True Friends of Africa—Not to the Philanthropists or to Exeter Hall.") Such animus and ridicule is an uneasy accompaniment to analysis, and Burton reveals the uncertainty, and the irrationality, of his position when he remarks on slavery both as an "evil" and as an "incal-culable boon to the black."

---

3 Richard Burton, *A Mission to Gelele, King of Dahome* (1864), ed. C. W. Newbury (London, 1966), 121, 215. Subsequent references are to this abridged edition.

4 *Mission to Gelele*, 201. In his official dispatch, Burton distinguished between the public execution of enemies and criminals and the "real sacrifices." "The real sacrifices," he wrote, "are secret, and these are fearfully frequent" (*Correspon-dence with British Ministers and Agents in Foreign Countries . . . relating to the Slave Trade* 56 [1865], No. 19, 23 March 1864, p. 21).

5 *Mission to Gelele*, 254.

In Dahomey itself, Burton displayed "hot passion and a harsh temper" rather than a "patient heart."[6] Such, at any rate, is the comment of the Reverend Peter Bernasko of the Methodist Missionary Society, who accompanied him. Burton refused to be kept waiting for King Gelele. He insisted on being accorded the same number of salutes that were given to Commodore Wilmot, a previous visitor. King Gelele's response to such behavior is itself indicated by Commodore Wilmot. In reporting to the Secretary of the Admiralty (7 August 1864), Wilmot forwarded a message from the King. "He did not like Burton," Wilmot reported, "and it was not likely he would make any treaty with him after refusing his friend the Commodore."[7]

It is not surprising, then, that Burton should have failed to persuade the King to turn from the slave trade and sacrificial practices. However, Burton can be credited with some success as an observer. For despite his predisposition and prejudice, which are clearly offensive to a reader today, his accounts of Dahomey provide some vivid description and probing analysis. Indeed, his book on Dahomey has been described in an authoritative work on the kingdom as "the most valuable of all the long series of works on Dahomey."[8] His reflections on the government of Dahomey are pointed—especially on the dual role of the King and the duplication of officers at court. He displays as well some understanding of the King's problematic position. In particular, he recognizes that the traditional sacrificial practices in Dahomey are related to filial respect and that the King was therefore not at liberty to turn from them. Such analysis—briefly introduced into the lecture—ensures that Burton's account is a characteristic mixture of traveler's tale and ethnological inquiry.

6　*Mission to Gelele*, 23.
7　*Correspondence with British Ministers*, 134.
8　Melville J. Herskovits, *Dahomey. An Ancient West African Kingdom* (1938; reprint, Evanston, Ill., 1967), 1:6.

Lecture 4
A Mission to Dahome

On the last occasion I had the honour and the pleasure of laying before you a short and imperfect statement of "What led to the Discovery of the Nile-Sources." Tonight you have kindly consented to accompany me upon an official visit to the King of Dahome, the Lord of the Amazons.

We thus shift the scene from East to West Africa, from the Somal who are free men and half caste Africans, to a typical Negroland Empire which may be called the head quarters of the Slave Coast.

But before beginning my journey perhaps you will permit me a few preliminary remarks upon that much vexed and little understood subject —the negro. Without entering into psychical or physiological minutiae I will briefly describe his so called "self-government," as observed in his own land by modern travellers, myself included.

Central Intertropical Africa, lying between north latitude 10° and south latitude 20°, contains at present eight considerable negro circles, which may be called kingdoms. Of these there are three on the west coast north of the Equator, namely:

1. Ashanti, the land which exports the "Minas" negroes. This despotism has been well known to us since the beginning of the present century. The capital is Kumasi, nearly 133 direct miles from the coast. This empire may be said to rest on two pillars, blood and gold. Human sacrifice is excessive, and the "customs" mean the slaughtering of fellow-creatures. For instance a daily victim is slain on the banks of the Holy River "Tando."

2. Benin, a kingdom well known to old travellers, and the place where Belzoni of the Pyramids died.[1] I visited it in August 1862 and my reception was the crucifixion of a negro. On the night after my arrival a second slave was slain and placed before my doorway. My lodgings commanded a view of the principal square, which was strewed with human bones, green and white.

3. Dahome. From the plain and unvarnished account of this tyranny, which I am about to offer, you will estimate the amount of hopeless mis-

---

1   G. B. Belzoni died while in quest of Timbuctoo. Burton described his visit to the
    supposed site of the grave in "My Wanderings in West Africa: a visit to the
    renowned cities of Wari and Benin," *Fraser's Magazine* (March 1863), 279.
    He wrote at length of the explorer in "Giovanni Battista Belzoni," *Cornhill* 42
    (July 1880): 36-50.

ery which awaits the African in Africa. And as it is unsatisfactory to point out a disease without suggesting a remedy, I will propose my panacea at the end of this lecture.

We now cross the Equator and find ourselves amongst the great South-African family. Their common origin is proved by their speech. Briefly to characterise their language, the place of our genders is taken by personal and impersonal forms, and all changes of words are made at the beginning, not, as with us, at the end. The Kafir (Caffre) race in South Eastern Africa is evidently a mixed breed, and it has nearly annihilated the Bushmen and the Hottentots—the original lords of the land. There is a curious resemblance between the Coptic, or Old Egyptian, and the Hottentot tongues, which suggests that in prehistoric ages one language extended from the Nile-Valley to the Cape of Good Hope. The true negroes, distinguished by the long, ape-like head, the projecting jaws, bowed shins and elongated heels and forearms, are all the tribes of Intertropical Africa whose blood is unmixed. This is my definition; but on this point opinions differ.

And here we may stand to view a gleam of light which the Future casts across the benighted Regions of the Dark Continent. Slowly but surely the wave of Moslem Conquest from the North and the East rolls down towards the Line. Every Moslem is a propagandist, and their traders, unlike ours, carry conversion with them. This fact European missionaries deny, because they do not like it: they would rather preach to Heathens than to Moslems, whom Locke described as unorthodox Christians. They even deny the superiority of El Islam, which forbids the pagan abominations of child-murder, human sacrifice, witch-burning, ordeal-poisons, and horrors innumerable. But we who look forward to the Advent of a Higher Law, of a nobler Humanity, hail with infinite pleasure every sign of progress.

In Southern Africa beginning from the Line we have 5 despotisms, namely:

1. Unyoro, or Kitwara, lately explored by Captains Speke and Grant, after I had published notices of it collected from the Arabs of Central Africa. For the horrors committed by Mwana Kamrasi, its cowardly and traitorous king, I may refer you to the printed works of those travellers.[2]

---

2 For Burton's account of Unyoro, see "The Lake Regions of Central Equatorial Africa," *Journal of the Royal Geographical Society* 29 (1859): 289-96. Speke's account is in *Journal of the Discovery of the Source of the Nile* (Edinburgh, 1863), chapters 17 and 18. James Grant's account is in *A Walk across Africa or Domestic Scenes from my Nile Journal* (1864), chapter 12.

2. Uganda, first visited by the same expedition. It is a land of abomi-nations, and the executioners are of the highest nobility. The King's sisters become his wives: the coronation-ceremony ends with burning to death some of the ruler's brothers; the courtiers are subject for the least offence to be cut to pieces with slips of sharp-edged grass [sic]; the subjects crawl like worms before their monarch, and to be murdered by him is almost an honour.

3. Karagwah, a small and powerless hill-Kingdom which is less cruel than its neighbours. Still we read that when the old King Dagara died, his body was deposited on the hill Noga-Namirinzi, where, instead of putting him underground the people erected a hut over him, and thrusting in five maidens and fifty cows enclosed the doorway in such a manner that all died of starvation.

4. Uropoe, or the Empire of the Mwata ya-Nvo. Here the royal death is an anthropological curiosity. Joaquim Rodriguez Graça, the Portuguese explorer, who visited it in 1843, gives the following account of it.[3] The King must die by violence: when he lives too long he is invited to make war and is suddenly deserted by his army. He takes the hint and, dressing in full costume, he sits upon the throne and calls all his family around him. His mother kneels at his feet, he beheads her and in due turn he slays his sons, his relations, and his wives, ending with the Arrakulle or favourite. Then an officer of the Court cuts off the royal legs and arms at the joints, and finally decapitates his master; upon which he is instantly put to death in the same way. This is indeed barbarism gone mad!

5 and last. Lunda, the Kingdom of the Mwata Cazembe: it was explored in 1798 by the learned Paulista, Dr de Lacerda, who died at the Capital.[4] This rule is more destructive of life than Ashantee or Dahome. As usual amongst negroes no man departs this life except by sorcery, a crime visited with fearful tortures. Prisoners of war are sacrificed to the muzimos or manes of the chiefs. The King when in a bad temper beats

---

3   Graça published *Viagem con destino as cabeceiras do rio Sena*, an account of his exploration of the Zambesi, in 1843. In "Lake Regions of Central Equatorial Africa," Burton described Graça as "a Portuguese merchant" who "penetrated deep into the unknown Continent" (p. 25).

4   In 1873, the Royal Geographical Society published *The Lands of Cazembe*, a translation by Burton of Dr. Francisco José de Lacerda's journal. Of the place name, Burton wrote that "it is variously pronounced Lucenda, Luenda, and by the Arabs Usenda, the difference being caused probably by dialect or inflexion" ("Lake Regions," 255n).

the drum "Chambançua" and whoever approaches him becomes a victim. It is certain destruction to touch a woman of the seraglio, even by accident. The introduction of a new wife into the royal harem is the signal for many deaths: indeed this is carried to such excess, we are told, that the jealous often use it as a pretext and wreak their vengeance upon the objects of their hatred.

After this, you will wonder with me at the following assertion made by that distinguished traveller Dr Livingstone (p. 522). "Though cheerless enough to a Christian," he remarks, "the African religion is mild in its character. In one very remote and small corner of the country, called Dahomey, it has degenerated into a bloody superstition. Human blood there takes the place of the propitiatory plants which are used over nine-tenths of the continent (!). The reckless disregard of human life, mentioned by Speke and Grant, is quite exceptional (!). We have heard from natives that a former possessor of Matiamvo's chieftanship was subject to fits of similar blood thirstiness, but he was clearly insane; and the great reverence for royalty, with which the Africans are imbued, alone saved him and probably Speke's Chieftan, Mtesi, also from decapitation."[5]

It is only fair to believe that Dr Livingstone wrote what he deemed the truth and to ascribe the gross mis-statement to the traveller's ignorance of Africa beyond the Zambezi River and S. Paulo de Luanda. Had the assertion come from a man of less simple faith I should have deemed it a pious fraud, and an attempt to throw powder in the eyes of the British Public with a view of extracting in favour of missionary enterprise more £.s.d. from the breeches-pocket of the easily plundered Mr John Bull.

The eight nations above alluded to are all composed of slave races, and most of them exported their chattels. Abolitionists sometimes still assert that the demand for servile labour in the New World originated slavery in Africa. But from time immemorial Northern and Eastern Africa have shipped their produce to Europe and Asia. Possibly in West Africa the export trade has caused more wars amongst the natives than took place before it was established—*more* wars but *fewer* deaths. I say

---

5 *Narrative of an Expedition to the Zambesi and its tributaries . . . 1858-64* (1865).
   Burton was frequently critical of Christian missionaries and remarked in
   Abeokuta and the Camaroons Mountains (London, 1863) on Livingstone's "usual
   peremptory and unsatisfactory way of laying down the law upon every
   question" (1:203).

possibly, because war amongst Africans as amongst all savages and barbarians is the normal state of man. Hunting and fighting are his sole excitements, his out of doors amusements, his races, his steeple chases. Africa has ever been a stage for conflicts of kites, of crows, of ignoble razzias [military expeditions] and commandos. And as long as wealth consists in slaves for the field and for the house, so long will the poor and hungry tribe fall upon and plunder its rich neighbours. I say also that if the wars have increased the deaths have diminished. When the African can sell his Captives for exportation he does so: if not he kills them unless wanted for use. Moreover his sensible style of transportation is to make money by his felons; he does not hang his criminals if he can put them to a better use. During my four years of penal servitude on the West Coast of Africa [as consul at Fernando Po, 1861-64], I was offered hundreds of men with the condition that they should be taken out of the country. The orders of Philanthropy compelled me to refuse the gift and the wretches doubtless died miserable deaths.

But if I proceed in this style you will inevitably determine me to be a slaver. In Brazil whenever I talk to negroes, they look knowingly at one another, they shake their heads, they mouth "Sabe nossa terra" and they depart convinced that I also have traded in "Casimir noir." Unwilling that this distinguished assembly should think so ill of me, I will offer a few words upon the subject of the "patriarchal institution."

Philanthropists, whose heads are sometimes softer than their hearts, have summed up their opinion of slavery as the "sum of all villainies." I look upon it as an evil, to the slaveholder even more than to the slave, but a necessary evil or, rather, a condition of things essentially connected, like polygamy, with the progress of human society, especially in the tropics. The savage hunting tribes slave for themselves; they are at the bottom of the ladder. Advancing to agricultural and settled life, man must have assistants, hands, slaves. As population increases, commerce develops itself and free labour fills the markets; the slave and the serf are emancipated: they have done their task; they disappear from the community, never more to return. Hence every nation, Hindu and Hebrew, English and French, have had slaves; all rose to their present state of civilisation by the "sum of all villainies." And here, when owning slavery to be an evil, I must guard against being misunderstood. It is an evil to the white man: it is an incalculable boon to the black. In the case of the negro it is life, it is comfort, it is civilisation. In the case of the white it has done evil by retarding progress, by demoralising society, and by giving rise to a mixed race.

And there is yet another point to be stated when speaking of the negro. In the United States every black man is a negro, or, to speak politely, a "cullurd pussun." Thus the noble races of Northern Africa and the half-Arab Moors, the Nubians and Abyssinians, and the fine Kafir (Caffre) type of South-eastern Africa are confounded with the anthropoid of Sierra Leone, of the Guinea, and of the Congo regions. The families first mentioned differ more from the true negro than they do from the white man.

Again the several African nations have been so long isolated that they have acquired marked characteristics, moral as well as physical. In Brazil many tribes are incorrectly massed under one name. For instance the proud fierce and intractable Ashantis, the Coromantyns and Winnebahs, the lazy, cowardly and false Fantis and Accas not to mention many others are called "Minas" from the old exporting centre S. Jorge d'Elmina. Again the "nagos," a corruption of "anago," the peoples north of Dahome Proper, embraced the tribes of the Yoruba or "Oyo" Empire, the latter numbering eight independent Kingdoms with an area of 50,000 square miles and a population of two millions.[6] The Egbas and Ekos are both Nagos: the former are pagans and agriculturalists, whose despotism gives them peculiar powers of combination, and much addicted to human sacrifice which they call the "basket offering." The latter are almost all Moslems, fisherman and traders, in fact the opposite of their neighbours. "Nago" moreover includes the people of Great Benin, of Dahome, and of the two Popos. In the 16th century flourished the Congo Empire, whose ruler, the "Manikongo," counted his banzas or towns by thousands. There are many excellent descriptions of his rule and customs, but it is well not to read them before going to bed. In Brazil the people of Luango, Angola, Casanji, and a multitude of other states are all called "Congos." The same is the case with the Benguelas.

My first visit to Gelele, King of Dahome, who now I believe entitles himself "Simekpwen," was in May and June 1863. Already in 1861 I had proposed to restore those amicable relations which we had with his father Gezo; but my application was not accepted by the Government. On my return to the West African coast after a six weeks' visit to Eng-

---

6　On a facing page, Burton specifies the following eight kingdoms: "Eko (by us called Lagos), Egba, Iketu, Ijshu, Ijsha, Efou, Ilvrin, and Yoruba Proper."

land, the journey was made on my own responsibility, and it was not pleasant. I was alone—in such matters negroes do not count as men—and four mortal days upon the Slave-Coast lagoons, salt, miry rivers, rich only in mud, miasma, and mosquitoes, with drenching rains and burning suns playing upon a cramping canoe without awning, are unsatisfactory even to remember. Having reached Whydah, the seaport and slave-market of Dahome, I procured a hammock, and in three days I arrived at Kana, a summer residence for the Court, distant seven and a half miles from Agbome, the capital.

The human sacrifices called the "Nago customs" had lately ended. Twelve men had lost their lives, and, dressed in various attire like reapers, dancers, and musicians, had been exposed on tall scaffolds of strong scantling.[7] "C'est se moquer de l'humanité," remarked to me the Principal of the French Mission at Whydah. But the corpses had been removed, and during my flying visit of five days nothing offensive was witnessed.

At Kana I met M. Jules Gérard, first "le chasseur," then "le tueur des lions": we had sailed together from Europe to Madeira, and he had been sea-sick during the whole voyage.[8] Men who have spent their youth in the excitement of dangerous sport often lose their nerve in middle age. This was the case with the unfortunate lion-hunter; the sight of the "customs" threw him into a fever. Disappointment also weighed upon his spirits. He came to West Africa in the hope that his fame as a killer of lions had preceded him but the only lion that can exist in that mouldy climate is the British lion, and even he is not a terrible beast to bring amongst the ladies. He expected to find Dahome a kind of Algiers, and he exchanged a good for a very bad country. He had set his mind upon crossing the northern frontier; but the king at once put a stop to that plan, and afterwards played me the same trick. He had also based his hopes upon his good shooting and upon an explosive bullet calculated to do great execution. But many of the king's women guards could use

---

7   These "customs" commemorated the victory of King Gezo, the predecessor of
    King Gelele, over the Oyos earlier in the century. In *Mission to Gelele*, Burton
    remarks: "The victims are made to personate in dress and avocation Oyos, a
    pastoral and agricultural people" (p. 126).
8   Jules Gérard described his experiences in Dahomey in a letter to the Duke of
    Wellington which was published in *The Times* (London), 18 August 1864.
    Burton included this letter, together with corrective footnotes, in an appendix to
    Mission to Gelele, 2:411-12. "The letter is interesting," Burton remarked,
    "as giving the darkest view of things Dahoman" (p. 412).

their guns better than he did, and when the said shell was produced, Gelele sent to his stores and brought out a box-full.

M. Gérard proposed to himself a journey which would have severely tried the health of the strongest man in Europe. He resolved to make his way from the Gulf of Guinea through dangerous Timbuktu (Timbuctoo) and the terrible Sahara to Algiers. I advised him to retire to Teneriffe or Madeira and to recruit his energies. But he was game to the last. He made another departure through the malarious Sherbro country, south of pestilential Sierra Leone. The next thing we heard of him was that when crossing the Jong River he had been drowned by the upsetting of a canoe. Somewhat later came the report that he had been foully murdered. I was rejoiced to hear that a subscription had been made for his aged and bereaved mother.

Having reported that Dahome was, under normal circumstances, as safe as most parts of Africa, I received in August 1863 orders to visit it as Commissioner. My "mission" was to make certain presents to the King, and to preach up cotton and palm oil versus war and human sacrifices. I may begin by assuring you that I lectured hard and talked to the wind.

H.M.'s cruiser "Antelope" landed me at Whydah in December, the dry season, and the surf was not particularly dangerous. The beach is open; between it and Brazil rolls the broad Atlantic; and near the shore are an outer and inner sandbar with an interval forming a fine breeding-ground for sharks. A girl is occasionally thrown in as an offering to "Hu," the sea-god, and this does not diminish the evil.

We entered Whydah in state, preceded and surrounded by chiefs and soldiery in war dress, kilts and silver horns like the giraffe's: their arms were long guns and short swords for decapitating the wounded. Each troop had its flag, its umbrella, and band of drums and tom-toms, its horns and cymbals. I especially remarked a gourd bottle full of, and covered with, cowries, or pebbles—in fact the celebrated "maracá" of Brazil, which, it has been conjectured, contributed towards the formation of the word "America." Every five minutes the warriors halted to drink and dance. The drink is easily described—tafia or bad caxaça [rum]. But the dance! I defy mortal man to paint it in words. Let me briefly say that the arms are held up as if the owner were running, the elbows being jerked so as nearly to meet behind the back; the hands paddle like the paws of a swimming dog; the feet shuffle and stamp as if treading water; the body-trunk joins in the play, and the hips move backwards and forwards to the beating of time. The jig and the hornpipe are repose compared with this performance. There is also a decapitation dance over an ideal dead enemy, whose head is duly sawn off with the edge of the hand.

At Whydah I lodged in the English Fort, a large double-storied build-ing of "taipa," tenanted by Wesleyan missionaries.[9] It was once a strong place, as the ruined towers and burst guns show.

There are three other Forts in the town. The Brazilian, which is near-est the sea, was held by Chico de Souza, the son of the late Francisco Fellis de Souza. This was a remarkable man. Born at Cachoeira, near Bahia, he emigrated to Africa, where by courage and conduct he became the "Chachá," or Governor of Merchants, a kind of Board of Trade. He made an enormous fortune, and by his many wives he left about a hun-dred olive branches. Though a slave-dealer, he was a man of honour, of honesty. The English had done him many an injury, yet he was invari-ably courteous and hospitable to every English traveller. He strongly opposed human sacrifice, and he saved many lives by curious con-trivances. Of the same stamp was M. Domingo Martins of Bahia, once celebrated for enormous wealth. He died in the interval between my first and second visits. I regretted his death, for he had been most kind and attentive to me.

The Portuguese Fort had also been repaired, and was inhabited by six members of the Lyons Mission, the "Vicariat Apostolique de Dahome." They kept a school, and they were apparently convinced that it was hopeless to attempt the conversion of adults. The superior, Father Francois Borghero, had several times been ill-treated by the barbarians, and his hatred of idolatry had exposed him to not a little danger. It is rare in those lands to find a highly educated and thoroughly gentlemanly man; and, looking back, I am not surprised that all my time not occupied by study or observation was spent in the Portuguese Fort.

Lastly there is the French Fort, in far better condition than the others. It was held in my time by M. Marius Daumas, agent to M. Régis (Aîné) of Marseilles, and *faute de mieux* he was buying and shipping palm oil.[10]

---

9   In *Mission to Gelele*, Burton defined this mud composition as the "national adobe" (1:66). He also related it to "the pise of Britanny and puddle of England, found from Devonshire via Dahome and Sindh, &c to Australia" (*Highlands of Brazil* [London, 1869], 1:102n).

10 Régis of Marseilles began legitimate trade at Whydah in 1841, while also dealing with slave traders as an importer. By 1851, the company had established a virtual monopoly in palm oil trading.

Whydah is easily seen. The houses are of red "taipa" with thick thatch, and each has its large and slovenly courtyard. The market-place is a long street of small booths open to the front, where everything from a needle to a moleque (small slaveboy) may be bought. The thorough-fares are studded with small round roofs of grass, which shelter a hideous deity called Legba. He is made of ruddy clay, with holes for eyes and cowries for teeth, and he squats before a pot in which the faithful place provisions, which are devoured by the urubú (vulture).[11] The chief temple is dedicated to the Danh, or snake, here the principal "fetish." It is a circular hut with two doorless entrances, and the venerated boas curl themselves comfortably on the thickness of the wall. The largest was about six feet long, and it is dangerous only to rats, of which it is very fond. Several foreigners have been killed for injuring these reptiles, and Whydah, once an independent kingdom, lost her liberty through the snakes. When attacked by Dahome in 1727, her chief defence was to place a serpent on the invaders' path. The Dahomans killed the guardian genius and slaughtered the Whydahs till the streets ran blood. But, when the conquerors had reduced their neighbour, they gave him leave to adore the snake, and Whydah felt consoled, even happy.

You must think that I am telling a traveller's tale.

I am talking history.

At Whydah we complied with the custom of sending up a messenger to report our arrival. After three days came two officials from the Palace, who presented their sticks and delivered to me a verbal invitation from their master. The sticks are white sticks, two feet long, adorned with plates of thin silver, cut into the shapes of lions, sharks, crocodiles, and other savage beasts. These batons serve as visiting cards, and are signs of dignity. When the King made me honorary commandant of a corps of life-guardswomen, he sent me two sticks by way of commission or diploma.

We set out en route for the capital on December 13, 1863. My little party consisted of Mr. John Cruikshank, a naval Assistant-Surgeon detached to accompany me; the Revd. Mr. Bernasko, Wesleyan mission-ary and private friend of the King; two negro interpreters, thirty ham-mock men, and a troop of baggage porters. This made up a total of

---

11 In *Mission to Gelele,* Burton elaborates on the "phallic worship" connected with Legba. "The figure is at squat," he writes, "crouched, as it were, before its own attributes. . . . The peculiar worship of Legba consists of propitiating his or her characteristics by unctions of palm-oil" (pp. 68-69).

ninety-nine mouths, which, allow me to say, were never idle except when asleep.

Between the seaboard and Kana, the "villegiatura," or country capital, of the King, there are fifty-two to fifty-three direct miles. The country is here a campo, or rolling grassy prairie: there a dense and magnificent forest. I have been reminded of it on the road from Campinas to Limeira in the Province of Sao Paulo. At every few miles there are settlements, now villages, once capitals which felt the weight of the Dahoman arm. The first is "Savi," ancient metropolis of the Whydah Kingdom, when the present Whydah, which is properly Gle-hwe, or the Garden House, was only a squalid port. The territory was only thirty miles by seven, but it mustered 200,000 fighting men. This, however, is easily explained. In Africa every male between the ages of seventeen and fifty carries arms: this would be about one-fifth of the population; consequently there was one million of inhabitants in an area of two hundred square miles (4,762 souls to each mile).

After Savi came Tevi [Toli], also an ex-capital. It is now a pretty little village commanded by a Dahoman "caboceer." This frequently used word is a corruption of a Portuguese corruption, "caboceire," or, rather, "caboceira," and means a headman, or a chief officer. The "etiquette" on arriving at such places is as follows. You alight from your hammock before the tree under which the grandee and his party are drawn up to receive you with vociferous shouts, with singing, drumming, and dancing. After the first greetings you pledge him in fresh water, which he has tasted before you. Then you drink spirits and receive an offering of provisions. You make a return of rum and gin, the people drum, dance, sing, and shout their thanks, and you are at liberty to proceed.

On the fourth day we crossed the "Agrimé Swamp," which is hardly practicable in the wet season. The road then entered upon a true continent: we emerged from the false coast, which at one time was under water, and which is raised by secular upheaval. At the little town of Agrimé we were delayed till the king, who was in his country capital, sent us an escort and permission to advance.

On Friday, December 18, we entered Kana, a large and scattered town, shaded by magnificent trees. It is about 270 feet above sea-level, and the climate was a relief after Whydah. The morrow was fixed for our reception. It was "Ember Day," and the date could hardly have been better chosen.

You can hardly form an idea of the *peine forte et dure* attending the presentation in Africa. It is every negro's object to keep the white man waiting as long as possible, and the visitor must be very firm and angry if he would not lose all his time.

We were duly warned to be ready at 10 a.m.; but local knowledge kept me in the house till 1 p.m. Then riding in handsome hammocks we sat under a tree upon the chairs which we had brought from Whydah, to witness the procession of "caboceers." Each grandee, preceded by his flag or flags, his band of drums and rattles, and his armed retainers dancing and singing, passed before us, shaded by an enormous umbrella of many colours. Having marched round, he came up to us and snapped his fingers (the local style of shaking hands); then he drank with us three toasts, beginning with his master's health. After the "caboceers" trooped various companies—musicians, eunuchs, and jesters. The latter are buffoons, reminding one of our feudal days. Their entertainment consists in "making faces" (*cara feia*), as children say—wrinkling the forehead, protruding the tongue, and clapping the jaws as apes do. They can tumble a little and "throw the cart wheel" neatly; they dance in a caricatured style, draw in the stomach to show that they are hungry, pretend to be deaf and dumb, smoke a bone by way of a pipe, and imitate my writing by scratching a sweet potato with a stick.

The Review over, we made for the Palace in a long procession; my men, wearing bright red caps and waist-cloths, carried the flag of St. George. The royal abodes are all on the same pattern: enclosures of "taipa" wall, five courses high, and pierced with eight or ten gates: the irregular square or oblong may be half a mile in circumference. At the principal entrances are thatched sheds like verandahs, one hundred feet long by fourteen to fifteen feet deep. The roof ledge rises sixty to seventy feet high, enough for two stories, whilst the eaves of thick and solidly packed straw rest upon posts barely four feet tall. The inner buildings, as far as they can be seen, correspond with the external, and the king holds his levees in one of these barn-like sheds. The royal sleeping-places, which are often changed, were described to me as neat rooms, divided from the courtyard by a wall with a *chevaux de frise* of human jawbones. The floors are paved with the skulls of conquered chiefs, forming a *descente de lit* upon which Gelele has the daily pleasure of trampling.

I must indent upon your patience whilst describing the complicated reception. It is typical of the Dahoman military empire.

We found, ranged in a line outside the gate, twenty-four umbrellas or brigades belonging to the highest male dignitaries. The army, or, what is here synonymous, the Court, is divided into two portions, male and female, or, rather, female and male, as the women troops take precedence. They occupy the inside of the Palace, and they are the King's body-guard in peace or war. Each line has a right and a left wing, so called from their position relative to the throne. The former, which is the senior, is commanded by the "min-gan" who cumulates the offices of Premier and Head-Executioner. His lieutenant is the Adanejan. Dahoman officials, for better espionage, are always in pairs. The General of the left wing is the "meu," who collects revenue and tribute, declares war, and has charge of all strangers. His *alter ego* is styled the Ben-wanton. Under these great men are smaller great men, and all were *de facto* as well as *de jure* slaves to the King.

Presently we were summoned to enter the palace. We closed our umbrellas by order, walked hurriedly across a large yard, and halted at a circle of white sand spread upon the clayey ground. Here we bowed to a figure sitting under the shady thatch; and he returned, we were told, the compliment. The chief ministers who accompanied us fell flat upon the sand, kissed it, rolled in it, and threw it by handfuls over their heads and robes of satin and velvet. This ceremony is repeated at every possible opportunity; and when the king drinks, all the subjects turn their backs upon him and shout.

Then we advanced to the clay bench upon which Gelele sat. After the usual quadruple bows and hand-wavings, he stood up, tucked in his toga, descended to the ground, and, aided by nimble feminine fingers, donned his sandals. He then greeted me with sundry vigorous wrings à la John Bull, and inquired after the Sovereign, the Ministry, and the people of England, which country is supposed to be like Dahome, but a little larger and richer.

Our chairs were then placed before the seat, to which he returned, and we drank the normal three toasts to his health. On these occasions it is not necessary to empty the glass, which may be handed to an attendant. Salutes having been fired, we retired a hundred feet from the presence and sat under giant umbrellas.

Gelele was then about forty-five years old, upwards of six feet high, olive complexioned, athletic and well made, with clear signs of African blood. His dress was simple to excess: a loose sheet of plain white stuff edged with green silk, a small straw smoking-cap, a few iron rings on his arms, and a human tooth strung round his neck. The only splendour was in his gold and scarlet sandals, here distinctive of royalty. They are studded with crosses, also regal emblems. He calls himself a Christian, and he is a Moslem as well: like all barbarians, he would rather believe too much than too little, and he would give himself every chance in both worlds.

Under the thatch behind the King were his wives, known by their handsome dresses, silver hair studs, and the absence of weapons. They atone for want of beauty by excessive devotion to their lord, who apparently does everything by proxy except smoke his long-stemmed clay pipe.

The inner Court of the Palace reflects the outer, and the women sit in the sun along the external wall of the royal shed with their musket-barrels bristling upwards. The right wing is commanded by a "Premieress," who also executes the women; the left is under the she "meu." A semicircle of bamboos lying on the ground separates the sexes at levées. The instrument of communication is a woman-messenger, who, walking up to the bamboos, delivers her message on all fours to the "meu." The latter proclaims it to the many.

I must here say a few words about the Amazons, or fighting women. The corps was a favourite with the late King, who thus checked the turbulence and treachery of his male subjects. You may have heard the number estimated at 10,000 to 12,000; I do not believe that it exceeds 2,500. They are divided into blunderbuss-women, elephant-hunters, beheaders, who carry razors four feet long, and the line armed with musket and short sword.

All the Amazons are *ex-officio* royal wives, and the first person who made the King a father was one of his colonelesses. It is high treason to touch them even accidentally; they lodge in the palaces, and when they go abroad all men, even strangers, must clear off the road. Gelele often makes his visitors honorary commandants of his guard, but this did not entitle them ever to inspect companies.

Such a *régime* makes the Amazons, as might be expected, intolerably fierce. Their sole object in life is blood-spilling and head-snatching. They pride themselves upon not being men, and with reason. The soldiers blink and shrink when they fire their guns; the soldieresses do not. The men run away; the women fight to the bitter end. In the last attack on the

The Amazon. From *A Mission to Gelele, King of Dahome* (1864).

city of Abeokuta (March 15, 1864) several of the Amazons of my own regiment scaled the walls; their brethren-in-arms hardly attempted the feat.

Dahome thus presented the anomaly of an African Kingdom in which women take precedence of men. Hence every employé of Government must choose a "mother"—that is to say, some elderly Amazon officer who will look after his interests at headquarters. Often he has two, an "old mother," dating from the days of the late king, and a "young mother," belonging to the actual reign. He must pay them well, or his affairs will be inevitably bad. Thus there is also a Brazilian, an English, and a French "mother"; and visitors of those nations are expected to propitiate their fond and unpleasant parents with presents of cloth, jewelry, perfumes, and so forth.

The levée ended with a kind of parade. A few simple manoeuvres and many furious decapitation dances were performed by a select company of young Amazons. They were decently dressed in long sleeveless waistcoats, petticoats of various coloured cottons, secured at the waist by a sash and extending to the ankles, whilst narrow fillets of ribbon secured their hair and denoted their corps. Their arms were muskets and short swords, and all had belts, bullet bags, and cartridge boxes.

When the sun set, a bottle of rum was sent to us. At this hint we rose and prepared to retire. Gelele again descended from his seat and accompanied us to the gate, preceded by a buzzing swarm of courtiers, who smoothed every inch of ground for the royal foot. He finally shook hands with us and promised to meet us in a few days at Agbome, the Capital.

We lost no time in reaching our destination and were surprised to find an excellent carriage-road, broad and smooth, between the two cities. Agbome has no hotels, but we managed lodgings at the house of the Bukono, a high officer who is doctor and wizard to the Court and curator of strangers, whom he fleeces pitilessly.

We are now about to witness the ill-famed "customs" of Dahome. The word is taken from the Portuguese "costume," and here means the royal sacrifices. Many travellers have witnessed them, but no one has attempted to inquire into their origin. Your patience will again be trespassed upon for a short time. You will not, it is hoped, be scandalized or look upon me as a propounder of paradoxes, when I attribute these murderous customs of our day not to love of bloodshed, but simply to filial piety.[12]

The Dahoman, like the ancient Egyptian, holds this world to be his temporary lodging. His true home is Ku-to-men, or Deadman's Land. It is not a place of rewards and punishments, but a Hades for ghosts, a region of shades, where the King will rule for ever and where the slave will for ever serve. The idea is perpetually present to the popular mind. When, for instance, sunshine accompanies rain the Dahoman says that the spirits are marketing. In Brazil the fox is marrying; in England the devil is beating his wife.

A deceased king therefore cannot be sent to Ku-to-men as a common negro. At his interment a small court must be slain—leopard-wives (that is to say, young and handsome wives), old wives, ministers, friends, soldiers, musicians, men and women. These are the Grand Customs, which may average 1,000-2,000 deaths. The Annual Customs, which we were now to witness, reinforce the ghostly court and number from 80-100 head. But destruction of life does not end here. All novelties, such as the arrival of an officer in uniform, must be reported to the dead by the live king. A captive or a criminal is summoned, and the message is given to him. He is made to swallow a bottle of rum, whose object is to keep him in good humour, and his head is there and then struck off. Only on one occasion did the patient object to the journey, saying that he did not know the road of Ku-to-men. "You shall soon find it out!" cried the King, who at once decapitated the wretch without rum. If any portion of the message be forgotten, another victim must be despatched with it. A hard-hearted traveller calls this the "Postscript."

A Dahoman king neglecting these funeral rites would be looked upon as the most impious of men, and a powerful priesthood would soon send him to Ku-to-men on his own account. You now understand how hopeless was my mission. It may be compared without disrespect to

---

12 Burton is not accurate in remarking that other writers have not inquired into the origin of these customs. In *History of Dahomy* (London, 1793), Archibald Dalzel comments that the customs are "sanctioned by the immemorial practice of past ages, under the idea of performing a grateful oblation to the deceased" (p. xix). John M'Leod in *Voyage to Africa* and Frederick Forbes in *Dahomey and The Dahomans* also relate the customs to ancestral respect. Forbes writes: "Gezzo, we are assured, has no delight in human sacrifices, and continues these awful scenes solely out of deference to ancient national customs" (p. 32). In his copy, Burton has noted marginally: "True. And so his son."

memorialising the Vatican against masses for the dead. The king's sole and necessary answer was *non possumus*.

The customs began on December 28, 1863, and ended on January 25, 1864. They were of two kinds. The first were performed by Gelele, King of the City; the second are in the name of Addo-Kpon, ruler of the "bush," or country—also Gelele. The ruler of Dahome is thus double, two persons in one, and each has his separate palace and property, mothers and ministers, Amazons, officers, and soldiers. I have conjectured that the reason of this strange dual organisation is that the "Bush-King" may buy and sell, which the "City-King" holds to be below his dignity.

The description of a single "custom" will suffice. About midday on December 28, when summoned to the Palace, we passed through the market-place, and we found the victim-shed finished and furnished. This building was a long, wall-less barn one hundred feet long, the roof was a thatch covered with a striped cloth on a blood-red ground and supported by tree trunks. On the west was a two-storied tower, sixty feet high, with four posts in front of each floor. There were, for this occasion, twenty victims sitting on stools, each before his post, with his arms round it and his wrists lashed together outside it. The confinement was not cruel; each had a slave to flap away the flies, all were fed four times a day, and they were released at night. The dress was a long white nightcap and a calico shirt with blue and crimson patches and bindings. A white man would have tried to escape; these negroes are led like black sheep to slaughter. They marked time as the bands played, and they chatted together, apparently "quizzing" us. I may here remark that at my request the King released half of these men, and that not one of them took the trouble to thank me or to beg alms from me.

Hardly were we seated when Gelele, protected by a gorgeous canopy umbrella, came forth from the Palace with Amazons and courtiers in a dense, dark stream. Having visited his fetish gods, he greeted us and retired to his seat under the normal shed. As at Kana, his wives crowded together behind and the soldieresses ranged themselves in front. The ceremonies consisted of dancing, drumming, and distributing decorations —necklaces of red and yellow beads. There was fearful boasting about feats of past valour and bravery to come. About sunset the King suddenly approached us, and I thanked him for the spectacle. He then withdrew, and we lost no time in following his example.

Nothing could be poorer than this display: any petty Indian Rajah can command more wealth and splendour. All was a barren barbarism, and the only "sensation" was produced by a score of human beings condemned to death and enjoying the death show.

On the morrow I sent a message to the Palace, officially objecting to be present at any human sacrifice, and declaring that if any murder took place before me I should retire to the coast. The reply was that few were to be executed, that the victims would only be malignant war-captives and the worst of criminals, and that all should be killed at night. With this crumb of comfort I was compelled to rest satisfied. Hitherto gangs of victims cruelly gagged had been paraded before visitors, in whose hearing and often before whose sight the murders were committed. Something is gained by diminishing the demoralising prominence of these death scenes. It has lately been determined that the "customs" of England shall be performed within the prisons, and not further debase the mob of spectators.

The catastrophe took place on what is called the "zán nyá nyáná," or the evil night. At intervals we heard the boom of the death-drum announcing some abominable slaughter. It was reported that the King had assisted with his own hand the Premier-Executioner.

On the next morning we were summoned to the Palace, whose approach was a horror. Four corpses, habited in the criminal shirts and nightcaps, sat as though in life upon the usual dwarf stools. The seats were supported upon a two-storied scaffold made of four rough beams, two upright and two horizontal, and about forty feet high. On a similar but smaller erection hard by were two victims, one above the other. Between these substantial erections was a tall gallows of thin posts, from which a single victim dangled by his heels. Lastly, another framework of the same kind was planted close to our path, and attached to the crossbar, by fine cords round the ankles and above the knees, hung two corpses side by side and head downwards. The bodies, though stiff, showed no signs of violence: the wretches had probably been stifled.

At the south-eastern gate of the Palace we found freshly severed heads in two batches of six each, surrounded by a raised rim of ashes. The clean-cut necks were turned upwards, and thus the features were not visible. Within the entrance there were two more heads; all the bodies had been removed, so as not to offend the king.

Thus on Gelele's "evil night" twenty-three human beings had lost their lives. And this is but one act in the fatal drama called the "customs." It is said that an equal number of women are slaughtered within the walls of the Royal abode, and I have every reason to believe the report.

I was kept waiting for two months in this den of abominations before the King would enter upon public affairs. He was discontented with the presents sent from England, and he was preparing to attack a large Nago city—Abeokuta—where, by the by, he was signally defeated.

When my last visit to him took place he stubbornly ignored, even in the least important matters, the wishes of H.M.'s Government. Filled with an exaggerated idea of his own importance, and flattered almost to madness by his courtiers, he proceeded to dictate his own terms. His next thought was an ignoble greed for presents. He bade me a friendly adieu, and asked me to visit him next year with an English carriage and horses, a large silk pavilion, and other such little gifts. I refused to promise, and I resolved not to put my head for the third time into the hyaena's mouth. For although Gelele has never shed the blood of a white man, he might, at the bidding of his Fetisheers, send a new kind of messenger to Ku-to-men by means of a cup of coffee or a dish of meat.

Such, ladies and gentlemen, is the delectable land of Africa. Such are the pleasures of negro society, the joys of native liberty, the comforts of the African home! This is the life, this is the death to which the amiable philanthropist would condemn his "black brother."

The stoppage of export slave-trade adds largely to the miseries of the negro—I now state the results of my personal experiences. Wars still continue in the interior and captives are sold to the coast-people engaged in the ground nut and palm oil traffic. The man fetches only a few shillings, provisions are enormously expensive; it pays therefore to starve and work to death the hand in a few months and to buy another. In this barbarous system the so called civilized black who calls himself a "native gentleman" has highly distinguished himself, and none more than the petted people of Sierra Leone and the British protégés generally.[13]

In slave-exporting kingdoms like Dahome the number of victims will be doubled. The checks upon human sacrifice are at present the hope of sale and a slight wish to humour Christian natives by taking as few lives as possible. Remove these obstacles to murder and you will restore the status quo of the "good old times" when hundreds of human beings instead of dozens lost their lives.

---

13 Africans liberated from slave vessels by the British were settled at Sierra Leone.

What then is to be done for Africa? To what progress can we look forward, now that we propose to remove the Squadron and to abolish the mixed Commission Courts?[14]

If any one imagines that I propose to restore the Export Slave-trade, he is greatly in error. Civilization cannot step backwards. Amongst all Christian nations compulsory labour is confined to criminals and where slavery exists it is an inheritance left by the necessities of past generations. The Export Slave-trade is dead; we cannot nor do we wish to see its resurrection.

But the negro cannot improve in his own country and it is a mercy to remove him from it. Again, in the interests of humanity it is unwise to leave the great African labour-bank without a draft. The world, especially the tropical world, is not yet habitable for mankind. It wants cleaning, sweeping, airing. And for this purpose what labourer is better than the African, the only savage who can live in the presence of the civilized man? The hour is fast approaching, I believe, when a free emigration from the benighted shores of Africa shall take the place of forced exportation. And to this measure I look forward as one conducing to the interests of both black and white.

The experiment of a free African emigration has, you will say, been tried and has failed. But the trial was no trial: it was the old slavery under a new name—writ larger.[15] I do not deny that many difficulties beset the subject, especially in the present age when the sweets of the slave-trade linger on so many African & European palates. It is however my conviction that the "Coolie" emigration both of India and China is not more easily regulated than that of Africa might be.

---

14 The British Squadron patrolled the coast in an attempt to stop the slave trade. The squadron was being called into question, owing to its cost, the difficulty of patrolling effectively, and the danger of offending foreign nations. The mixed commission courts (or Equity Courts) were made up of African chiefs and supercargoes with an elected chair. The courts met monthly to hear grievances, lay fines, and fix duties. Burton was responsible for revising court procedures in May 1862, but he admitted that "all signed the agreement but no one adhered to it" (*Mission to Gelele*, 11).

15 The primary reference is to the scheme of Régis in the 1850s to send out "indentured" laborers from Whydah to the French Antilles. In "Lake Regions of Central Equatorial Africa," Burton also remarks briefly on the disguised continuation of slavery. "It is hoped," he notes, "no honest man's mental vision can be so obfuscated as to be incapable of discerning the old evil, through its disguise of a new name" (p. 19). Burton also criticized Régis's procedures and related schemes of the 1840s in *Two Trips to Gorilla Land*, 2:313-15.